Share Capital

Share Capital

Professor Andrew McGee, MA, BCL (Oxon), Barrister
Professor of Business Law and Director of the Centre for Business Law and Practice, Leeds University

The University of Leeds Company Law Series

Butterworths
London, Edinburgh and Dublin
1999

United Kingdom	Butterworths, a Division of Reed Elsevier (UK) Ltd, Halsbury House, 35 Chancery Lane, LONDON WC2A 1EL and 4 Hill Street, EDINBURGH EH2 3JZ
Australia	Butterworths, a Division of Reed International Books Australia Pty Ltd, CHATSWOOD, New South Wales
Canada	Butterworths Canada Ltd, MARKHAM, Ontario
Hong Kong	Butterworths Asia (Hong Kong), HONG KONG
India	Butterworths India, NEW DELHI
Ireland	Butterworth (Ireland) Ltd, DUBLIN
Malaysia	Malayan Law Journal Sdn Bhd, KUALA LUMPUR
New Zealand	Butterworths of New Zealand Ltd, WELLINGTON
Singapore	Butterworths Asia, SINGAPORE
South Africa	Butterworths Publishers (Pty) Ltd, DURBAN
USA	Lexis Law Publishing, CHARLOTTESVILLE, Virginia

A CIP Catalogue record for this book is available from the British Library.

ISBN 0 406 90069 8

Typeset by M Rules, London
Printed by Hobbs the Printers Ltd,Totton, Hampshire

Preface

The complex nature of company law is well-recognised, as is its tendency to grow at an alarming rate. An academic colleague calculated some years ago that if the growth in company law regulation continues unabated, then by the year 2047 the entire earth's surface will be covered in it. Even if this prediction remains unfulfilled, it seems safe to say that there is and will continue to be a need for books which deal in detail, yet lucidly and concisely, with particular areas of the subject. It was with this need in mind that this series was conceived. The books in the series, of which this is one of the first, are intended to offer to both academics and practitioners a new understanding of and insights into this fascinating yet frustrating area of the law.

Share capital was chosen as one of the first topics both because of its obvious importance and because it has been somewhat neglected in recent years. This book aims to pull together company law rules from various different parts of the Companies Acts and to show how they relate to each other as well as how they work in practice. Much of the material covered is detailed and technical, yet all the rules have an underlying rationale; once this is understood, many apparently obscure provisions suddenly become comprehensible.

I have to thank Gary Scanlan of the City University, who read through the entire manuscript. I should also acknowledge the often unwitting contributions of delegates at many CPD conferences over the years who have listened patiently to my expositions of my views on this subject. The editorial staff of Butterworths have, as ever, been keen and efficient in handling the manuscript. My wife Judith and my daughter Grace (who is now old enough to know that she appears in the prefaces of her father's books) have, as ever, provided essential support and encouragement.

The law is stated as at 1 January 1999.

Andrew McGee
January 1999

Contents

Table of statutes

References to Statutes are to Halsbury's Statutes of England (Fourth Edition) showing the volume and page at which the annotated text of the Act may be found.

References in the right-hand column are to paragraph number.

Table of cases

PARA

O

P

Q

R

S

PARA

Y

Chapter 1

Principles of share capital

THE NOTION OF SHARE CAPITAL

1.1 The notion of share capital may be said to lie at the heart of company law (though of course it is one of the many fascinations of the subject that from alternative points of view other concepts, such as corporate personality or directors' duties or even at the present day the rights of minority shareholders, might be made plausible candidates for this honour). It is the fact of having a share capital at a structural level that distinguishes the typical company[1] from any unincorporated body. The opportunity to divide up the ownership rights in a company in this way is an important source of flexibility for a company, not least because it allows a separation between ownership and control which is not so easily achieved in an unincorporated body. This separation has been one of the great successes of modern capitalism, allowing businesses a relatively simple way of soliciting venture capital from the public at large, and thus allowing that same public to share in the rewards of successful enterprise.

1 Although it is possible to have a company limited by guarantee without a share capital, such entities are rare at the present day.

1.2 At the same time, the system of share capital is by no means free of difficulty, as can readily be confirmed by a glance at the contents of the Companies Act 1985 ('CA 1985'). Parts IV, V and VI of that Act are entirely to do with share capital. Part IV is headed 'Allotment of Shares and Debentures'. Part V is headed 'Share Capital, its Increase, Maintenance and Reduction'. Part VI is headed 'Disclosure of Interests in Shares'. These three Parts of the Act together make up ss 80–220. In addition, Part XV (ss 454–457) deals with 'Orders Imposing Restrictions on Shares'. Sheer quantity of provisions should not be confused with importance, but a detailed examination of those provisions will readily show the extreme importance of the matters covered, as well as revealing the difficulties which arise from them.

THE CAPITAL MAINTENANCE DOCTRINE

1.3 The capital maintenance doctrine forms the basis of the company law rules relating to the share capital of the company. The basic doctrine may be shortly stated, though discussion of its ramifications and exceptions will require discussion in greater detail.

History of the doctrine

1.4 The doctrine of capital maintenance is that the paid-up share capital of a company forms a permanent fund available to the creditors of the company to meet their legitimate claims against the company. It is therefore not to be dissipated by the company, nor must it be returned to the shareholders, whether in the guise of dividends or otherwise.

1.5 The doctrine was established by the House of Lords in *Trevor v Whitworth*[1] where shareholders in a company had purported to sell some of their shares to the company, which had not paid the purchase price in full. The shareholders sued for the balance, but the House of Lords unanimously held that the transaction was not valid. Unfortunately, two distinct lines of reasoning were employed. The first rested on the fact that the company's memorandum contained no power to repurchase shares (though the article laid down procedures for making such repurchases). It was therefore said that the purported repurchases were ultra vires and thus void. Such a view accorded perfectly well with the very strict rule on ultra vires contracts which the House of Lords had adopted 12 years previously in *Ashbury Railway Carriage and Iron Co Ltd v Riche*[2], but is obviously out of line with modern company law. Although it would by itself have been enough to dispose of the particular case, it would not have been of fundamental company law importance, since it could easily have been circumvented by including an express power to repurchase in the memorandum.

1 (1887) 12 App Cas 409.
2 (1875) LR 7 HL 653.

1.6 The more general point also taken by the House of Lords was that a company cannot repurchase its shares at all, since it does so either to reduce its capital, which goes against the principle that the capital is available as a permanent fund for creditors, or to traffic in the shares, which was regarded as inherently unlawful. On the one hand it is obviously true to say that the capital of a company is intended to have some function, and there are attractions in saying that this sum, the amount of which is of course a matter of public information, should form a permanent fund. The doctrine no doubt seemed especially attractive in the 19th century, when courts were still working out their attitudes to these new-fangled creations, limited companies, and when the general view was the activities of companies needed to be severely controlled[1]. Unfortunately, the doctrine is difficult to accept as a practical reality at present. Companies commonly use their share capital, in conjunction with their other assets and funds for the purpose of operating the business (it would be odd if they did not) and at any given time – but especially in the early days of a new business – it may well happen that the company has no available funds to meet creditors' claims. This is especially the case where the issued capital is relatively small, as it often is in the case of a private company. It does not follow that the company is being mismanaged, nor that creditors are necessarily prejudiced. In *Trevor v Whitworth* Lord Herschell expressly recognised this possibility, but without appearing to realise that it rather undermines the notional purpose of the capital maintenance rule. There is also the point that creditors are prejudiced only to the extent that they know what the issued capital is. Many creditors in fact never know this, and those who give credit after the reduction have in any event the chance to be aware of it if it matters to them[2].

1 This attitude may be regarded as being responsible for such decisions as *Ashbury Railway Carriage and Iron Co Ltd v Riche* (1875) LR 7 HL 653 (ultra vires contracts void) and *Re German Date Coffee Co* (1882) 20 Ch D 169 (company wound up for failure of substratum).

2 The distinction between existing creditors and subsequent creditors no doubt underlies the rules in CA 1985, ss 135 ff about protecting existing creditors in the event of a court-authorised reduction.

1.7 It would have been possible to argue that the ratio decidendi of *Trevor v Whitworth* was the narrow one that a company could not repurchase its shares unless authorised to do so by its memorandum, but in fact it came to be accepted that the broader ratio, ie that repurchase was contrary to the notion of a company was the one to be followed. Strict adherence to this rule eventually came to be seen as inconvenient, not least in small companies, where repurchase of the shares by the company is often the best way of buying out a shareholder who wishes to leave[1], and the doctrine was significantly relaxed by the Companies Act 1981, the relevant provisions now being consolidated in CA 1985, ss 159–181.

1 Farrar *Company Law* (4th edn, 1998) at pp184–5.

Subsidiary holding shares in parent

1.8 There is a general prohibition in CA 1985, s 23 against a subsidiary company holding shares in its parent company. This is imposed to prevent the situation of company A controlling company B which in turn has shares in company A. Such a state of affairs is both practically inconvenient and a potential infringement of the capital maintenance doctrine, since the same capital could in effect be used to purchase both sets of shares. However, there is no general prohibition on cross-shareholdings between two companies, neither of which is a subsidiary of the other. This applies whether or not both companies are subsidiaries of a common parent. Section 23 provides that any allotment or transfer of shares in a company to its subsidiary is void. This does not deal with the situation where the subsidiary holds shares in the parent company before it becomes a subsidiary of the parent[1]. Section 23 appears to forbid the existence of such shareholdings, but equally fails to impose any sanction if the subsidiary fails to divest itself of the shareholding. Nor is it easy to see what sanction could be imposed. The logic of s 23 presumably requires that the transfer of the shares to the subsidiary be avoided ab initio, but this is most unlikely to be considered a satisfactory solution, given that the transfer may have happened some time in the past and may have been made in complete good faith. The avoidance would also allow the purchaser to recover the purchase price on the basis of a total failure of consideration. It is submitted that this is a simple lacuna in the law, and that there is in fact no sanction for retaining the shares in these circumstances.

1 As in *Acatos & Hutcheson plc v Watson* [1995] 1 BCLC 218.

1.9 The prohibition does not apply where the subsidiary holds the shares only as personal representative or trustee (so long as the company is not a beneficiary under the trust)[1]. Nor does it apply where the subsidiary holds the shares purely as a marketmaker[2]. In any of these situations an examination of the location of the relevant beneficial interests will show that there is no infringement of the general principles which CA 1985, s 23 is designed to uphold.

1 CA 1985, s 23(2).
2 CA 1985, s 23(3).

Structure of the subject

1.10 The topic of Share Capital may conveniently be divided into a number of areas, as follows:

Minimum share capital requirements
Creation of share capital
Rights attached to shares
Issue of shares
Transfer of shares
Removal of shares.

The first two of these are dealt with in the remainder of this Chapter. The others are outlined here, before being dealt with in detail in the subsequent Chapters.

Minimum share capital requirements

1.11 Given the importance which company law attaches to the maintenance of a company's capital as a creditor protection device, it would seem reasonable to expect that companies would be required to have a certain minimum level of capital before being permitted the privilege of incorporation. In fact English law has never had any minimum capital requirement for private companies. Until 1980 there was no minimum capital requirement for public companies, and even in 1980 the requirement was introduced only in respect to an EC Directive[1] which required this to be done.

1 Second Company Law Directive – Directive 77/91/EC.

1.12 The basic requirement is now contained in CA 1985, s 117. Section 117(1) provides that a company originally registered as a public company is forbidden to do business or exercise any borrowing powers until the Registrar of Companies has issued it with a certificate under s 117 or it has been re-registered as a private company.

1.13 In order to obtain a section 117 certificate a company must satisfy the Registrar that its allotted share capital is not less than the authorised minimum and must deliver to the Registrar a statutory declaration complying with the requirements of section 117(3).

1.14 The authorised minimum is defined by CA 1985, s 118(1) as being £50,000 or such other sum as may be specified by statutory instrument. At present the figure still is £50,000; indeed, this figure has not changed since the requirement of minimum capital for companies was first introduced by the Companies Act 1980. Accordingly, it might well be regarded as being somewhat out of date, given the changes in the value of money which have taken place since then. Although the figure of £50,000 must be denominated in sterling[1], any share capital other than the authorised minimum[2] may be denominated in other currencies if the company so chooses[3]. There is apparently no reason why the capital cannot be denominated partly in one currency and partly in another.

1 It is thought that this may change once the Euro becomes an accepted currency. If the UK does ever join the Euro zone, then it will have to change.
2 And thus all the share capital of a private company.
3 *Re Scandinavian Bank Group plc* [1988] Ch 87.

1.15 Section 117(4) of the CA 1985, deals with the special position of shares allotted under an employees' share scheme. Such shares are not to be taken into account in determining the nominal value of the allotted share capital, unless paid-up to at least one quarter of its nominal value and the whole of any premium on it.

1.16 Section 118(2) of the CA 1985 makes further provisions in relation to an order increasing the authorised minimum. One obvious problem arising from an increase in the authorised minimum is that there may be existing public companies whose allotted share capital is, quite lawfully, more than the old authorised minimum but less than the new authorised minimum. Section 118(2) allows the order increasing the authorised minimum to require such companies to raise their allotted capital to the new minimum level or re-register as private companies[1]; it also allows the order to make provision for any of the matters with which the Act deals in relation to the registration, re-registration, change of name, payment for shares or offer of shares or debentures to the public. This includes making provision as to the consequences (civil or criminal) of failure to comply with any requirement of the order[2]. The order may also contain any necessary transitional and supplementary provisions[3].

1 CA 1985, s 118(2)(a).
2 CA 1985, s 118(2)(b).
3 CA 1985, s 118(2)(c).

1.17 The statutory declaration under CA 1985, 117(3) must be signed by a director or secretary of the company. It must do the following things:

(a) state that the nominal value of the allotted share capital is not less than the authorised minimum;

(b) specify how much of the allotted share capital has been paid-up at the date of the application;

(c) specify the amount or estimated amount of the company's preliminary expenses and say who has paid them or is liable to pay them;

(d) specify any amount or benefit paid or given, or intended to be paid or given, to any promoter of the company, together with the consideration for such payment or benefit.

The statutory declaration must also be in the prescribed form, which is laid down by the Companies Forms (Amendment) Regulations 1995[1].

1 SI 1995/736.

1.18 The Registrar is empowered (but apparently not required) to accept a statutory declaration under this section as sufficient evidence of the matters contained in it[1]. In practice such declarations are routinely accepted, and it is difficult to see what more the Registrar could legitimately request. A certificate issued by the Registrar is conclusive evidence that the company is entitled to do business and exercise borrowing powers[2]. This protects against the consequences of CA 1985, s 117(7) which imposes liability to a fine on the company and every officer of it who is in default in the event that the company does business or exercises borrowing powers without having the necessary certificate. It should be noted, however, that the section does not invalidate any transaction entered into by a company. The desire to protect innocent third parties has led to the enactment of section 117(8), which preserves the validity of such transactions, but with the gloss that the directors of the company become personally liable to indemnify the other party for any loss or damage caused the company's failure to perform its obligations within 21 days of being called upon to do so by the other party to the transaction.

1 CA 1985, s 117(5).
2 CA 1985, s 117(6).

1.19 At this point it is necessary for a moment to step out of the statutory order of sections and draw attention to CA 1985, s 101. This section applies only to public companies. If forbids a public company to issue a share unless it is paid up as to at least one-quarter of its nominal value and the whole of any premium on it. The rule does not apply to shares issued in pursuance of an employees' share scheme[1]. Where a share is allotted in contravention of s 101 the allottee remains liable to pay to the company the difference between the amount actually paid and the minimum amount which should have been paid, together with interest[2]. It appears from the statutory wording that this liability remains on the allottee (exclusively) even if the share is sold before the minimum amount has been paid. Section 101(3) confusingly provides that where a share is allotted in contravention of s 101, the share is to be treated as if one-quarter of its nominal value, together with any premium on it, had been received. This appears to mean that the validity of the allotment is not affected and that the share participates in rights to dividends, voting and capital as if there had been no irregularity. In other words the only sanction is that contained in s 101(4).

1 CA 1985, s 101(2).
2 CA 1985, s 101(4).

1.20 Section 101(3) and (4) of the CA 1985 do not apply to the issue of bonus shares unless the allottee knew, or ought to have known, that the shares were allotted in contravention of s 101(1)[1]. The only situation where the allotment of bonus shares could give rise to a s 101 problem is where the shares are allotted but the company fails to appropriate money from a reserve account or the profit and loss account to pay for them, at least as to the statutory minimum. The non-application of s 101(4) in such a case ensures that the allottee does not become liable to make up the deficit, as is logical, since it was always intended that the payment would come from the company's resources.

1 CA 1985, s 101(5).

1.21 The non-application of CA 1985, s 101(3) is more problematic, since it takes away the provision which preserved the normal share rights in such cases, and there seems no reason to do this. It is suggested that the answer to this problem is that s 101(3) is purely declaratory. If it had never been enacted there would have been no reason to suppose that an error in regard to the payment for the shares deprived the registered holder of his statutory rights. On this reasoning the disapplication of s 101(3) in relation to bonus shares was unnecessary and perhaps inappropriate, but has done no harm.

1.22 Although it is questionable whether at present the requirement to have a par value for shares serves any useful purpose, it remains part of the law, and there are apparently no plans to change it.

1.23 Section 119 of the CA 1985 is a declaratory provision which authorises the company to do a number of things in relation to its shares. It may on the issue of shares make arrangements under which different shareholders will pay up the capital on their shares at different times and in different proportions[1]. It is not usual to do this in public companies in relation to shares issued at a single time, but private companies do sometimes take advantage of the provision.

1 CA 1985, s 119(a).

1.24 The company may also accept from any shareholder the whole or part of an amount remaining unpaid on any shares he holds, even though no call has been made for money outstanding on the shares[1]. It seems likely that the company would have this power even in the absence of this provision, which may therefore be regarded as having been inserted for the avoidance of doubt.

1 CA 1985, s 119(b).

1.25 Finally, CA 1985, s 119 allows the company to pay dividends in proportion to the amount paid-up on shares where a larger amount is paid up on some shares than on others. This is another section which may be regarded as declaratory, but it does give rise to at least one interesting issue in its reference to 'amount' rather than 'proportion'. If a company has issued partly-paid shares on more than one occasion and with different total amounts due, it is possible that those with larger *amounts* paid-up might have smaller *proportions* of the total price paid-up. Yet s 119(c) of the CA 1985 only authorises payment of dividends in proportion to the amounts paid-up. Two points may be made. The first is that the point will be of no importance if it is true that the company is at liberty to determine the way in which it calculates dividend entitlement independently of s 119, since entitlement could then be calculated on the basis of proportion of total amount paid-up, relying on the general power to do this. The second point is that s 119 is fairly clearly not intended to deal with the situation here identified. It is meant to deal only with the case where all the shares concerned were issued at the same time and for the same price. In these circumstances calculations based on amounts paid up always produce the same result as calculations based on proportion paid-up, so that the issue discussed here does not arise. It is suggested that, although the wording of s 119(c) does not inevitably lead to this conclusion, the proper interpretation of the provision is that it has no application to the case where not all the shares whose entitlement is being compared were issued at the same time and for the same price. This interpretation removes one apparently anomalous result from consideration. However, it does not deal properly with the case where partly-paid shares have been issued at different times and for different prices. Indeed, it may make this case more difficult, since it follows that s 119 cannot be used to justify differential payments, so that some other argument will have to be found. It is here that one comes up against the curious lack of authority in the CA 1985 on the subject of dividend payments.

1.26 There is no provision in the Acts which requires the payment of dividends *pari passu* or on any other basis. Table A, arts 102–108 contain provisions for the declaration and payment of dividends. Article 104 reproduces and expands on the effect of CA 1985, s 119(c) (in particular the reference to the amounts paid up rather than the proportions paid-up); but it is a commonplace that these provisions can be removed from the articles if the shareholders see fit. The general proposition must be that the rights attaching to shares are those set out in the memorandum and/or articles of association.

1.27 In practice, however, details of this kind are frequently not dealt with expressly. In such circumstances it is presumably necessary to start from the idea that equality is equity, so that at any rate all fully-paid shares should participate in dividend equally unless the contrary is stated. The difficulty arises in relation to partly-paid shares. On the one hand the idea that shares which are less than fully-paid should have some reduction in their share entitlement seems entirely fair and reasonable. On the other hand, there have been some well-known share issues in public companies which have not operated on that basis[1]; in addition, there is still the problem of working out how the reduction should be calculated. It is suggested that the answer to this is that there is no reduction unless the articles authorise the making of a reduction. If the articles do so authorise, then their provisions are conclusive. However, it ought to be possible for the articles to authorise reduction based on proportion rather than on absolute amount. It is then to be noted that art 104 of Table A may be regarded as being unsuitable in its present wording. Finally, it is instructive to observe an important difference between CA 1985, s 119 and art 104. The former allows a company to pay dividends on this proportionate basis. It seems to assume that it is a matter for the directors to decide at the time when a dividend is declared. The latter requires payment on this basis, leaving the directors with no discretion. Of course it might be thought that the former solution is to be preferred because it promotes certainty and avoids any allegations of bias on the part of the directors. On the other hand the latter solution allows greater flexibility, and there might well be situations where it was to the company's advantage to make use of this flexibility. All this reinforces the earlier point that art104 is poorly drafted. Most companies would be well advised to exclude it from their articles of association. Either it should be replaced with a better piece of drafting which addresses both proportionality and discretion, or, perhaps better still, the dividend rights attaching to shares should be properly stated in the memorandum or articles in terms which make the point explicit and avoid any need to rely on s 119.

1 BT and TSB come to mind as relatively recent examples.

1.28 Section 120 of the CA 1985 deals with the reserve liability of a limited company. This provision, rarely used, allows a company to decide by special resolution that any portion of its share capital which has not been called up shall not be capable of being called up, except in the event of and for the purposes of the company being wound up. Section 120 makes explicit the effectiveness of such a resolution. This section has been in the law for many years[1] and may well have served a useful purpose in the days when directors had general powers to issue shares without regard to the views or interests of existing members. Given that this is no longer the case, and given that a resolution of this kind reduces the company's room for manoeuvre in a way which seems to confer few commercial advantages, it is hard to imagine why a company would wish to exercise the power contained in s 120 at present.

1 It was previously section 60 of the Companies Act 1948.

Increase of capital

1.29 Section 121 of the CA 1985 allows limited companies with a share capital (whether limited by shares or by guarantee) to make alterations to their share capital, if so authorised by their articles. Section 121(2) lists a number of specific things which the company may do. It may increase its share capital by new shares of such amount as it thinks expedient[1]. This is the aspect of s 121(2) which is most commonly used. It is the provision which allows for a general increase of share capital by a company which wishes to expand. A number of important points should be noted in relation to this paragraph. First, a resolution under this paragraph affects only the *authorised* capital of the company. It does not by itself effect an allotment of shares, nor is it a substitute for observing the requirements of authority to issue shares in s 80 or the pre-emption rights in s 89. It is additional to all these requirements. Second, this paragraph expressly contemplates the possibility that the new shares might have a different nominal value from the pre-existing shares. Third, although it does not expressly say so, the paragraph is treated as authorising the creation of shares of different classes, though of course that procedure would normally also requirement an amendment to the memorandum, where the rights attaching to shares are set out.

1 CA 1985, s 121(2)(a).

1.30 The company may consolidate and divide any or all of its share capital into shares of larger amounts than its existing shares[1]. It appears that this paragraph is rarely used. It might occasionally be convenient to consolidate existing shareholdings in this way, but one side-effect of so doing is that the shares tend to become less marketable, since the value of any given share is necessarily increased.

1 CA 1985, s 121(2)(b).

1.31 The company may convert all or any of its paid-up shares into stock, and re-convert that stock into paid-up shares of any denomination[1]. At the present day this provision appears to be redundant, not least because the Companies Acts contain no definition of 'stock'. However, it is suggested that what this paragraph effectively does is to allow the company to re-configure its share capital without changing the total amount of share capital. From this point of view the use of 'stock' may simply be regarded as an administrative convenience.

1 CA 1985, s 121(2)(c).

1.32 The company may sub-divide its shares, or any of them, into shares of smaller amount than is fixed by the memorandum[1]. This is the converse of **1.17** (b) above and is rather more commonly used. It is especially appropriate where the value of the shares has increased greatly since their original issue and it is now desired to make them more readily tradable by splitting them into more manageable blocks. If this option is taken at a time when some of the shares are less then fully-paid, then the proportion between the amount paid and the amount unpaid on the reduced shares must be the same as it was on the shares from which the reduced shares have been created[2]. As this requirement is contained in the CA 1985 rather than in Table A, and is not expressed to be subject to contrary provision, it appears to be mandatory.

1 CA 1985, s 121(2)(d).
2 CA 1985, s 121(3).

1.33 The company may cancel shares which, at the date of the passing of the resolution for cancellation, have not been taken or agreed to be taken by any person. The company's share capital is thereupon diminished by the amount of the shares cancelled[1], but this does not constitute a reduction of share capital within the meaning of CA 1985, s 135[2]. This is because that section is intended to deal with the breach of the capital maintenance doctrine inherent in reducing the amount of the *paid-up* capital. A cancellation of unissued shares does not have that effect. In modern circumstances it is hard to see why any company would want to take this option. Even if the directors see no point in issuing shares for the time being, there is no obvious reason to foreclose the possibility of issuing them at some future date if circumstances change. If shareholders are concerned that the directors may issue the shares in inappropriate circumstances, they should ensure that there is no s 80 authority in force to permit an allotment. They might also do well to remember that the power to allot shares is a fiduciary power and, like other fiduciary powers of the directors, must be exercised bona fide and in the best interests of the company.

1 CA 1985, s 121(2)(e).
2 CA 1985, s 121(5).

1.34 The power given to the company under CA 1985, s 121 must be exercised by the company in general meeting[1], though as with other general meeting powers, this must be read subject to the possibility of written resolution, either under the elective regime or in a particular case even though the elective regime generally is not in force for the company at the time. Since s 121(4) says nothing about which kind of resolution is required for the exercise of powers under s 121, it is to be assumed that an ordinary resolution suffices.

1 CA 1985, s 121(4).

1.35 Sections 122 and 123 of the CA 1985 make further provision for giving notice to the Registrar of various changes. Section 122 applies to conversions of shares into stock and vice versa, to sub-divisions of shares, to redemptions of redeemable shares (even though this topic is not dealt with by s 121) and to cancellations of unissued shares. Section 122(1) requires that notice of the changes made be given to the Registrar within one month of the making of the changes. Failure to comply is a regulatory offence: the company and every officer of it who is in default become liable to a fine and a daily default fine for continuing contravention.

1.36 Section 123 of the CA 1985 deals with the case of an increase in the share capital. Notice of such an increase must be given to the Registrar within 15 days of the passing of the resolution for increase. The notice must include the prescribed particulars[1] in respect of the classes of shares affected and the conditions subject to which the new shares have been or are to be issued. Failure to comply is a regulatory offence: the company and every officer of it who is in default become liable to a fine and a daily default fine for continuing contravention. The reference to showing the conditions on which the shares 'have been issued' clearly implies that the increase takes effect as soon as the resolution is passed, rather than when it is submitted to the Registrar, since otherwise it would be impossible to issue the new shares before the resolution was submitted; it would then be impossible for the shares to have been issued already.

1 The prescribed form is Form 123, authorised under the Companies (Forms) Regulations 1985, SI 1985/854.

Class rights

1.37 Sections 125–129 of the CA 1985 deal with the conditions under which changes made be made in the rights attaching to particular classes of shares. These questions are fully dealt with in Chapter 5.

Share premium account

1.38 Sections 130–134 of the CA 1985 deal with the situation where shares are issued at a premium to their nominal value. This topic is to be regarded as arising in relation to the issue of shares and is dealt with in Chapter 2.

Reduction of capital

1.39 Sections 135–141 of the CA 1985 deal with circumstances in which a company may reduce its issued capital. These sections are fully examined in Chapter 4.

Loss of capital

1.40 Sections 142–150 of the CA 1985 contain a number of important provisions implementing in detail the general principle that a company is required to maintain its share capital as a fund available to creditors. As these sections relate to the general doctrine of maintenance of capital, they are examined in detail here.

1.41 Section 142 of the CA 1985 applies only to public companies. It provides that where the net assets[1] of a public company are half or less of its called-up share capital the directors are required to convene an Extraordinary General Meeting for the purpose of discussing what steps, if any, should be taken to deal with the situation. The meeting must be called within 28 days of the first day on which the situation is known to any director of the company and must be held within 56 days of that day. The section appears to require actual, rather than merely constructive, knowledge in order to set this period running. Where the meeting is not duly called, each director who knowingly and wilfully authorises the failure to call the meeting, or after the expiry of the 18 days knowingly and wilfully authorises or permits the failure to continue, commits an offence punishable by fine[2].

1 There is no definition of this given in the section, but it is to be presumed that the usual definition of assets less liabilities will apply.
2 CA 1985, s 142(2).

1.42 Section 142(3) of the CA 1985 goes on to provide that nothing in s 142 authorises the consideration at a meeting called in pursuance of s 142(1) of anything which apart from s 142(1) could not properly have been considered at that meeting.

1.43 This section is in some respects less effective and significant than might at first appear. First, it does not require the company to take any action to remedy the loss of capital; although a meeting must be convened, it is perfectly possible for that meeting to decide that no action is possible, or appropriate, or necessary. Indeed, the limitation in CA 1985, s 142(3) on the powers of the meeting convened under s 142(1) makes it only too likely that this will happen. Second, and perhaps more seriously, the section does nothing to impose upon directors any duty to monitor the state of the net assets so as to be aware that this loss of capital has occurred. The duty to convene the meeting arises only when a director is actually aware of the situation. Moreover, the penalty for non-compliance with the obligations imposed by the section is relatively trivial. Finally, it may be suggested that there will in any event be very few instances in which the section is likely to be of practical importance. It would be a very negligent board of directors which failed to notice the seriousness of the company's position long before the level of net assets fell as low as 50% of the called-up share capital. Perhaps the one situation where the section could plausibly be expected to be relevant is that where the company suffers a large loss from a single transaction, so that the net assets are reduced very suddenly.

Prohibition on acquiring own shares

1.44 Section 143 of the CA 1985 imposes a general prohibition on a company acquiring its own shares. Such acquisition obviously reduces the share capital of the company and thus reduces the fund available to creditors. The prohibition applies to acquisition by purchase, by subscription or otherwise (ie acquisition by any means). If a company purports to act in defiance of this prohibition, the company is liable to a fine, and every officer of it who is in default is liable to a fine or imprisonment or both[1]. Perhaps most important of all is the final part of s 143(2), which provides that the purported acquisition is void. Although the Companies Act 1985 gives no further guidance as to the consequences of this voidness, these consequences may be deduced by logic. In the case of a purported acquisition by subscription, the shares must remain unissued. In the case of a purported acquisition by purchase, the shares must continue to belong to the party who owned them immediately before the purported transfer.

1 CA 1985, s 143(2).

1.45 Section 143(3) of the CA 1985 goes on to list exceptions to the general prohibition. These are:

(a) redemption or purchase under the provisions on buyback of shares[1];

(b) acquisition of shares in a reduction of capital duly made;

(c) purchase of shares in pursuance of an order of the court under ss 5[2], 54[3];

(d) or Part XVII[4] of the CA 1985.

1 CA 1985, ss 159–181; see Chapter 5.

2 Alteration of objects.
3 Litigated objection to re-registration of public company as private.
4 Unfair prejudice provisions; CA 1985, ss 459–461.

1.46 Despite the prohibition of CA 1985, s 143, there is apparently no general rule against a company issuing shares to a person who will hold them as nominee for the company, nor against a person acquiring shares in a company as nominee for that company. In such circumstances the nominee would become the registered holder, and the principle that the register is conclusive as to ownership would preclude any further enquiry into the beneficial title to the shares. However, at least one problem area remains. Section 145 of the CA 1985 deals with the situation where shares in a company are issued to or acquired by a nominee of that company as partly paid-up. The problem which must be dealt with in this case is that of the liability to pay for the shares. To this end, s 144(1) provides that the shares are to be treated as held by the nominee on his own account and that the company is to be treated as having no beneficial interest in them. Consequently, liability to pay calls for any sum outstanding on the shares must rest elsewhere. Section 144(2) provides that the liability rests initially with the nominee, but adds further provisions in case the nominee fails to pay within 21 days of being called upon to do so.

1.47 Where the shares were issued to the nominee as a subscriber to the memorandum and in pursuance of an undertaking of his in the memorandum, then joint and several liability to pay is also imposed on each of the other subscribers to the memorandum[1]. Where the shares are issued to or acquired by the nominee in any other circumstances, then the joint and several liability is imposed on each of the directors of the company at the time of the acquisition[2]. However, this liability is subject to the provisions of s 144(3), (4).

1 CA 1985, s 144(2)(a).
2 CA 1985, s 144(2)(b).

1.48 The former of these subsections applies in proceedings for the recovery of sums due under s 144. It empowers the court to relieve a subscriber or director against liability under s 144 if it appears that he has acted honestly and reasonably and, having regard to all the circumstances of the case, ought fairly to be excused from liability. The latter subsection applies in circumstances where a subscriber or director has reason to apprehend that will or might be made for the recovery of sums due under s 144. He may then apply to the court for an order relieving him against liability, and the court has the same power to grant such relief as it has under s 144(3).

1.49 Section 145 of the CA 1985 contains provisions restricting the application of s 144. Section 145(1) disapplies s 144(1) (but not the other parts of s 144) where a nominee acquires shares in a public company with the aid of financial assistance from that public company and the company has a beneficial interest in the shares. The significance of this appears to be only that in these circumstances the fiction that the company has no beneficial interest in the shares is not applied. Section 145(2) disapplies s 144(1), (2) in the case of shares acquired by a nominee of a company when the company has no beneficial interest in those shares. Although s 144(3), (4) are not expressly disapplied, the point is of no practical significance, since these two subsections are relevant only in cases where there might otherwise be liability under s 144(2), which clearly cannot happen in cases to which s 144(2) does not apply.

1.50 Sections 146–150 of the CA 1985 make special provision in relation to shares held by or for a public company. Section 146(1) lists the circumstances in which the section applies:

(a) where shares in the company are forfeited, or surrendered to the company in lieu, in pursuance of the articles, for failure to pay any sum payable in respect of the shares;

(b) where the nominee of the company acquires shares in the company from a third person by any of the methods mentioned in s 143(3) (which lists the ways in which a company may lawfully acquire its own shares);

(c) where the nominee of the company acquires shares in the company from a third person without financial assistance being given directly or indirectly by the company and the company has a beneficial interest in the shares;

(d) where a person acquires shares in the company with financial assistance given to him directly or indirectly by the company for the purpose of or in connection with the acquisition, and the company has a beneficial interest in the shares.

1.51 Where the section applies, there is a limit on the length of time for which the company may retain the shares or any interest in them[1]. The period is three years from the date of acquisition in cases falling with (a), (b) or (c) above, and one year from the date of acquisition in cases falling within (d)[2]. If the company fails to dispose of its interest in the shares by the end of the relevant time, it must cancel them and diminish its share capital by the nominal value of the shares cancelled. If this has the effect of reducing its allotted share capital below the authorised minimum[3], then it must apply for re-registration as a private company, stating the effect of the cancellation.

1 CA 1985, s 146(2).
2 CA 1985, s 146(3).
3 CA 1985, s 117 – £50,000.

1.52 Section 147 of the CA 1985 allows the directors to take the necessary steps to comply with these requirements without going through the capital reduction procedure is ss 135 ff. Thus they may pass a resolution altering the memorandum so that it no longer states that the company is a public company and make any other alterations requisite in the circumstances[1] (it appears that this is a case where the memorandum may be altered by a resolution of the directors, rather than a resolution of the company in general meeting).

1 CA 1985, s 147(2).

1.53 The application for re-registration as a private company must be in the prescribed from under the Companies (Forms) Regulations, must be signed by a director or the secretary and must be delivered to the Registrar with a printed (not photocopied) copy of the memorandum and articles as altered by the resolution[1]. The Registrar considers whether the company is eligible to be re-registered under CA 1985, s 146. If the is satisfied that it is, the retains the application and issues the company with a new certificate of incorporation in a form appropriate to its new status. The company thereupon becomes a private company, and the alterations to the memorandum and articles take effect accordingly. The certificate is conclusive evidence that the requirements of ss 146–148[2] have been complied with in relation to the re-registration, and that the company is a private company[3].

1 CA 1985, s 147(3).
2 For CA 1985, s 148; see para **1.2.8** below.
3 CA 1985, s 147(4).

1.54 While the shares are held by the company or its nominee, no voting rights may be exercised in respect of them, and any purported exercise of those rights is void[1].

1 CA 1985, s 146(3).

1.55 Section 149 of the CA 1985 imposes sanctions for non-compliance with s 146(2). Section 149(1) imposes what may be regarded as a civil sanction, namely that once the period for disposing of the shares has expired, the company is subject to s 81 (restriction on public offers) as if it were a private company, even if it has not yet re-registered. However, in all other respects s 149(1) provides that the company continues to be treated as a public company. Section 149(2) imposes criminal sanctions for failure to cancel shares or to apply for re-registration when required to do so under s 146(2). The company and every officer of it who is in default is liable to a fine and for continued contravention a daily default fine.

Effect of re-registration as plc[1]

1.56 Section 43 of the CA 1985 sets out a procedure by which a private company which has a share capital may be re-registered as a public company. Sections 44 and 45 then deal with certain consequences of re-registration in relation to shares and share capital.

1 CA 1985, ss 44–45.

1.57 One of the requirements for re-registration under CA 1985, s 43 is that the company must submit to the Registrar a balance sheet for the company, which must have been prepared to a date not more than seven months prior to the date of the application for re-registration[1]. Section 44 of the CA 1985 applies in the situation where shares have been allotted by the company between the date at which the relevant balance sheet was prepared and the passing of the special resolution under s 43, and those shares were allotted fully or partly-paid as to their nominal value or any premium on them otherwise than in cash[2]. Where s 44 applies, the

Registrar is not allowed to accept the application for re-registration unless the consideration for the allotment of the shares has been valued in accordance with s 108 of the CA 1985[3] and a report with respect to the value of the consideration has been made to the company within the six months immediately preceding the allotment of the shares[4] (not the date of the application for re-registration).

1 CA 1985, s 43(3)(c) and 43(4).
2 CA 1985, s 44(1).
3 CA 1985, s 108.
4 CA 1985, s 44(2).

1.58 There are a number of exceptions to the application of CA 1985, s 44(2). It does not apply to the extent that the consideration for the shares has come from amounts standing to the credit of the company in any of its reserve accounts or in its profit and loss account[1]. This provision is likely to work well enough where all the consideration has come from these sources. However, where only part of the consideration is exempted by s 44(3) it appears, on the basis of principle and by careful reading of the statutory words, that the part of the consideration which has not come from these sources is still subject to the valuation and reporting requirements of s 44(2).

1 CA 1985, s 44(3).

1.59 Section 44(4) of the CA 1985 provides a further exception to s 44(2). It applies where the allotment of shares is made under an arrangement (including, but not limited to an arrangement under s 425 of the CA 1985[1] by which the consideration is to be the transfer to the company (or the cancellation) of some or all of the shares of another company Although this is obviously a case of non-cash consideration, s 44(2) is excluded, provided that participation in the arrangement is open to all the holders of shares (or shares in the affected class of shares) in the other company[2]. Section 44(6) provides a further exception where the allotment of shares is made in connection with its proposed merger with another company.

1 CA 1985, s 44(7).
2 CA 1985, s 44(5).

1.60 Section 45 of the CA 1985 goes on to impose further share capital requirements in connection with the re-registration of a private company as a public company. These are intended to ensure that by the time of re-registration the company complies with the same requirements as are imposed on a new company which is to be incorporated as a public company. Thus, the nominal value of the company's authorised share capital must be not less than the authorised minimum[1] and each of the company's allotted shares must be paid up as to at least one quarter of the nominal value and the whole of any premium on it[2].

1 CA 1985, s 45(2)(a); for the authorised minimum see CA 1985, s 117.
2 CA 1985, s 45(2)(a).

1.61 If any shares in the company have been allotted fully or partly-paid or any premium on them has been discharged by any undertaking by any person to do work or perform services (for the company or for another) then the undertaking must have been performed or otherwise discharged[1]. The rather curious wording of this provision appears to leave open the possibility that the undertaking could be 'discharged' if the company simply released the other party from the performance of it. This might reasonably be thought to be objectionable on the ground that it would mean that the company received no value for the shares which it had allotted.

1 CA 1985, s 45(3).

1.62 There are two possible answers to this point. The first is that the release of the undertaking is not a 'discharge' within the meaning of this provision, since it is necessary that the work shall actually have been done by someone (not necessarily the person who gave the original undertaking). The second possibility is to say that in the particular context of CA 1985, s 45 there is no objection to allowing the undertaking to be released. On this argument the purpose of s 45 is to ensure that at the time of re-registration there is as little uncertainty as possible about the company's level of assets. If the undertaking has been released, then it is clear that its value is nil, so there is no uncertainty. Of course there would be other questions for the directors as to whether it was a proper exercise of their powers to release the undertaking, but those questions do not arise under s 45 and are not relevant here.

1.63 The latter argument has distinct attractions, not least that it can be adopted without doing violence to the statutory words. However, some confusion is then injected into the argument by a consideration of s 45(4). This subsection applies where shares have been allotted and the consideration consists of or includes an undertaking to the company other than one to which s 45(3) applies, ie where the undertaking is for something other than doing work or performing services, such as the transfer of an asset to the company. In this event the undertaking must have been performed or discharged or there must be a contract between the company and some person under which the undertaking is to be performed not later than five years from the date on which the resolution for re-registration under s 43 is passed[1].

1 CA 1985, s 45(4).

1.64 Given that s 45(4) of the CA 1985 adds the extra option of a contract for the performance of the undertaking at some future date, it is necessary to ask why this option is included and how this relates to the arguments rehearsed above about the notion of 'discharge' of an undertaking. If the reason for the requirement of performance or discharge is to clear away uncertainties as to the value of assets, then it would not seem appropriate to allow the substitution of a contract to perform the undertaking at some date in the future. It might be thought that such a contract would be less problematic where the undertaking is not for work or services (which are notoriously difficult to value in any objective way) but from the point of view of valuation it may also be said that the value to the transferee of a contract to transfer an asset depends on the value of the asset, and there are significant assets (not least land) the value of which is prone to fluctuate according to extraneous circumstances. Consequently it might well be difficult to value a contract of this kind. In the absence of authority it is obviously not possible to come to a clear view about the ambiguities of s 45(3), (4), but it is suggested that the release of an undertaking should in principle not be accepted as a 'discharge' for these purposes, bearing in mind that s 45 forms one of the provisions of the CA 1985 which attempt to ensure that the real value of the share capital of a company is maintained at the time when it changes its status from private to public.

1.65 Section 45(5), (6) of the CA 1985, deal with the disregard of certain shares for the purposes of determining compliance with the rules in s 45(3), (4) as well as with the rule that all shares must be at least one-quarter paid-up. Shares which are to be disregarded for these purposes are firstly those allotted before 22 June 1982 (up to a maximum of one-tenth of the nominal value of the company's allotted share capital[1] not including employees' share scheme shares disregarded under the next provision) and secondly those allotted in pursuance of an employees' share scheme which would otherwise preclude the company from being re-registered as a public company solely because of non-compliance with the requirement that shares be at least one-quarter paid-up.

1 CA 1985, s45(6).

1.66 Section 124 of the CA 1985 deals with unlimited companies which have a share capital and which seek re-registration as public companies under CA 1985, s 43 or as private companies under s 51. The resolution for effecting such re-registration may do the same as a resolution under CA 1985, s 120 or may increase the nominal capital by increasing the nominal amount of each of the company's shares, but subject to the condition that no part of the increased capital is to be called up except in the event and for the purpose of a winding up. Nothing further need be said about the former possibility, but the latter calls for more comment. It is more likely to be used in the case of re-registration as a public company than in the case of re-registration as a private company.

1.67 Re-registration as a public company carries the possibility of needing to increase the value of the authorised capital in order to meet the minimum capital requirements of CA 1985, s 117. One way of doing this would be to increase the nominal value of each share. However, to protect existing shareholders from increased liability as a result of this option, the extra nominal value must be subject to call-up only in the event of winding up. Although the fact of this restriction does not have to be included in a statutory declaration under s 117(3), its existence would come to the attention of the Registrar and of anyone who searched the register because it would be part of the resolution for re-registration, which has to be filed[1]. Although at first sight this might be thought be a way of evading the minimum capital requirements, such an impression is misleading. Provided that the situation which a company reaches by taking this route is that of having an authorised capital of at least the minimum £50,000[2], with at least one-quarter of it paid-up, the intention behind the minimum capital requirements is not frustrated, and there is no reason to reject this technique.

1 CA 1985, s 43.
2 CA 1985, s 118.

1.68 Section 148 of the CA 1985 applies where there is a s 146[1] acquisition or surrender of shares in a private company, which is subsequently re-registered as a public company. In such a case, s 148 applies the provisions of ss 146, 147 and 149, except that the relevant period for the disposal of the interest in the shares runs from the date of re-registration as a public company rather than from the date of the acquisition of the interest[2].

1 For CA 1985, s 146 see para **1.2.7** above.
2 CA 1985, s 148(2).

Chapter 2

Issuing shares

FIRST SHARES

2.1 Every company must have at least one share in issue (and a public company must have at least two). Thus, the issue of the first share(s) is a matter which must be attended to before the company can be incorporated. However, this is a classic chicken-and-egg situation, since it is logically impossible for the company to issue shares before it comes into existence. The usual solution to this is for the subscribers to the memorandum to agree to take one share each. Whether that share is in fact ever issued to the subscriber after incorporation is another matter.

2.2 In cases where the company is formed by company professional agents or other legal professionals such as solicitors, it is quite common for the subscribers to the memorandum never in fact to become shareholders. This is a convenient practice, since it simplifies the transfer of the company to its eventual owners (especially if the happening of this is somewhat delayed, in which event the subscribers may no longer be available) but it does have the odd consequence that a company which has been duly formed may for some time have no actual shareholders. Of course this situation does not in practice give rise to any great difficulty, since shelf companies of this kind will only be in this situation while they are inactive.

2.3 As it is no longer necessary to have two shareholders in a private company[1] it is possible to issue just one share initially.

1 CA 1985, s 1(3A), inserted by the Companies (Single Member Private Limited Companies) Regulations 1992, SI 1992/1699, reg 2.

2.4 The issue of initial shares is obviously not subject to any form of pre-emption right, and initial shares should go to those who have agreed in the memorandum to take them, or to whoever is now intended to become a shareholder. The first directors will have been appointed at the time of incorporation, and it is presumably open to them to proceed with the allocation of initial shares as they see fit. Certainly the pre-emption rules cannot apply since there will be no one with existing shares which can be used as the basis for calculating the individual entitlements.

FURTHER SHARES

2.5 When considering the issue of further shares three sets of rules have to be considered, relating to authorised capital, directors' authority to allot and shareholders' pre-emption rights.

Authorised capital

2.6 The directors must check what is the authorised capital of the company and whether there is enough unauthorised capital to support the proposed issue. If not, the authorised capital should be increased by an ordinary resolution. Section 121 of the CA 1985 authorises the company to increase its capital in this way. The Ordinary Resolution is exceptional among OR's in the CA 1985 in that it requires to be filed with the Registrar.

2.7 The consequence of exceeding the authorised capital appears to be a complete mystery. No provision in the CA 1985 deals with this question in any way. The answer seems to depend upon what view is taken about the nature of share capital, and the question thus touches on some fundamental aspects of company law. On one view the position must be that any allotment in excess of the authorised capital is a logical impossibility, and that any attempt to make such an issue is simply void. Where the memorandum states, for example, that the capital of the company is '£1000 divided into 1000 shares of £1 each' (a fairly common level of capital for small private companies) there are only 1000 shares in existence. Since shares which do not exist presumably cannot be issued, it must follow that a purported allotment beyond this level is void. The argument is at first sight logical and attractive. Unfortunately, it gives rise to a number of practical difficulties.

2.8 Suppose a company has the kind of capital clause mentioned above. Suppose also that this company has issued 800 shares. The directors now, in disregard of the limitation on capital, issue a further 500 shares, 200 to A, 150 to B, 100 to C, 50 to D. The argument considered here would lead to the conclusion that not all these shares can be validly issued. But it would not lead to the conclusion that none of them was validly issued, since at the relevant time the company still had 200 shares available for issue. Assuming that the allotment was done by means of a single resolution of the board of directors (or even that it was done in a single meeting of the board of directors) the question inevitably arises, which 200 shares were validly allotted and which 300 were not validly allotted, there appears to be no satisfactory way in which this question can be answered. It might be possible to say that each of our four allottees gets 50 shares, or that the valid shares are divided up in proportion to the purported allotment, so that in the example given 40% of each shareholder's allotment is valid. However, either of these is an arbitrary and unsatisfactory solution.

2.9 The position becomes even more difficult where some time has elapsed since the improper allotment. Various other events may have intervened for example, allottees may have sold some of their shares. How is it to be decided whether the shares which they sold were 'genuine' or not? What if they have sold all their shares, but in parcels to different purchasers? Dividends may have been declared on the shares, which should never have been paid. There may have been general meetings at which votes have been cast on the shares. Accounts may have been prepared showing the company's share capital in accordance with the purported allotment. Presumably all these questions will have to be reopened (subject to any possible limitation defence, though it is not at all clear which of the sections of the Limitation Act 1980 would apply to such a case).

2.10 By now the chaotic consequences of holding the purported allotment to be void must be readily apparent, and it is therefore not surprising if company lawyers seek to avoid these consequences by adopting a different analysis of the purported allotment. The alternative analysis must rest on drawing a distinction between that which is improper but effective, and that which is simply ineffective. The distinction is of course well recognised in the law; indeed, as appears below, it is a distinction which is used in relation to allotments made by directors who are not duly authorised. According to this analysis, the allotment is not invalidated by the fact of exceeding authorised capital limits. There is no doubt that this analysis resolves all the difficulties alluded to earlier as flowing from the conclusion that allotments in excess of the authorised capital are void. The problem with the analysis is that it leaves the requirement of authorised capital with no sanction to back it up and thus, from one point of view, with no significance. This may appear a very serious drawback, but in fact in the modern law it may be a sensible conclusion.

2.11 The authorised capital requirement was originally included in order to protect shareholders against the irresponsible issue of new shares by the directors. The requirement of an ordinary resolution to increase share capital is intended to give shareholders some control over the process in the sense that the extent of further issues is subject to their control. However, the rule was introduced at a time when directors had no need of further authority before allotting shares, ie when the provisions which are now ss 80–88 of the CA 1985 had no place in English law. Now that these provisions are part of the law, it is at least arguable that the authorised capital requirement serves no further purpose. On this basis it might well be argued that the lack of any sanction for breach of it is not a matter for concern.

Fettering the power to increase capital

2.12 In *Russell v Northern Bank Development Corpn Ltd*[1] as part of the restructuring of a company, an agreement (the restructuring agreement) was entered into between the company and its bankers and its senior executives, who held the entire issued share capital of the company. The restructuring agreement provided that no further share capital should be created or issued without the written consent of all the parties to the agreement. The company proposed to increase its share capital and the plaintiff, who was a party to the restructuring agreement, sought an injunction to prevent it from doing so on the grounds that this was in breach of the agreement. The judge held that the restructuring agreement constituted an improper fetter on the statutory power of the company to increase its share capital and as such it was unenforceable. The plaintiff appealed but the Court of Appeal upheld this view. It is not clear whether the resulting increase would be a breach of contract (though valid in itself) or whether by saying that the agreement was unenforceable the court meant to rule that no liability would arise from the increase. It is suggested that the former view is to be preferred.

1 [1992] BCLC 431, NICA.

2.13 Although it is not uncommon in company law to hold that companies may not effectively fetter their powers, it is usual in such cases to recognise the contractual nature of the purported fetter[1].

1 *Rusell v Northern Bank Development Corpn Ltd* [1992] BCLC 1016, HL; see also cases such as *Punt v Symons & Co Ltd* [1903] 2 Ch 506 and *Southern Foundries (1926) Ltd v Shirlaw* [1940] AC 701, HL; contra *Bailey v British Equitable Assurance Co* [1904] 1 Ch 374, CA; Farrar *Company law* (4th edn, 1998) at p132.

Authority to allot

2.14 Since 1980 there has been an additional requirement that directors proposing to allot shares must under certain circumstances have the authority of the members to do so[1]. The authority may be given by the company's articles or by the company in general meeting[2].

1 CA 1985, s 80.
2 CA 1985, s 80(1).

2.15 The requirement applies only to allotments of what the CA 1985 terms 'relevant securities'. These are all shares in the company other than shares shown in the memorandum to have been taken by the subscribers or shares allotted in pursuance of an employees' share scheme, together with any right to subscribe for or convert any security into shares in the company. Thus, in effect, CA 1985, s 80 applies to most allotments of shares after the initial allotment, the only material exception being that for employee share schemes, defined in CA 1985, s 743 as:

> '. . . a scheme for encouraging or facilitating the holding of shares or debentures in a company by or for the benefit of
>
> (a) the bona fide employees or former employees of the company, the company's subsidiary or holding company or a subsidiary of the company's holding company, or
> (b) the wives, husbands, widows, widowers or children or step-children under the age of 18 of such employees or former employees'

2.16 Authority given for the purposes of CA 1985, s 80 may be given generally or for the purposes of a particular allotment[1]. The authority must state the maximum amount of relevant securities which may be allotted under it and the date on which it will expire. This date must not be later than five years from the date of incorporation (where the authority is contained in the company's original articles) or from the date on which the resolution giving the authority is passed (where authority is given by resolution of the general meeting)[2]. The authority may be renewed or further renewed by the company in general meeting, but the resolution renewing the authority must state the number of relevant securities which may be allotted under it[3] (or the number remaining to be allotted in cases where some have already been allotted) and must state the date on which the renewed authority will expire[4].

1 CA 1985, s 80(3).
2 CA 1985, s 80(4).
3 Or, if the offer is of a right to subscribe for shares, the maximum amount of shares which may be allotted pursuant to that right; CA 1985, s 80(6).
4 CA 1985, s 80(6).

2.17 It appears that in practice many private companies deal with the problems of these provisions by including as a standard item in the business of the Annual General Meeting ('AGM'), a resolution authorising the directors to allot up to the current authorised capital for a period of five years from the resolution. This ensures that at any given time there is authority to allot for between four and five years, and the practice of making the extension of the authority a standard item on the agenda of the AGM should ensure that the authority is never allowed to lapse through oversight. On the other hand, this practice is capable of giving rise to at least two points of ambiguity in the interpretation of CA 1985, s 80, as well as being potentially dangerous for shareholders.

2.18 The first point of ambiguity concerns the position if the authorised capital is increased before an allotment is made but after the resolution has been passed. Presumably the intention is that the resolution should then retrospectively come to operate in relation to the new maximum authorised capital. However, it is open to doubt whether the section is intended to permit this. On the face of it there is nothing in CA 1985, s 80 which prohibits the resolution from naming a maximum allotment which would involve exceeding the authorised capital. This is a further reflection of the lack of linkage between the authorised capital rules and the authority to allot rules. It must, however, be seriously doubted whether an allotment in these terms could be valid. Where the authorised capital is subsequently increased, it might well be argued that authority to allot the increase requires a further positive act of the shareholders. This certainly seems to accord with the general principle of s 80 that directors should not be allowed to allot without shareholder authority. As against this, two arguments may be deployed. The first is that the matter can be adequately dealt with by proper drafting. If the s 80 resolution refers to allotment of the authorised capital 'for the time being' then it is implicit in the wording that this capital might later increase. The second argument, developing from the first, is that increases in the authorised capital require the approval of the shareholders in any event. It would seem a little odd that the shareholders are prepared to increase the authorised capital but not prepared to authorise the directors to allot it. This argument is of course even stronger if there is in place a s 80 resolution referring to the authorised capital for the time being.

2.19 The second difficulty arising from the practice of a five-year rolling authority concerns the wording of CA 1985, s 80(4), which requires that the authority state the date on which it expires. It is usual in such clauses to state that the authority is valid for five years from its date. Although this makes it a very simple matter to work out the date of expiry, a very pedantic approach to statutory interpretation might lead to the conclusion that the resolution is invalidated by the failure to mention the date. A simple practical solution to this is to amend the drafting so as to mention the date. From the point of view of interpretation it should also be borne in mind that s 80 was introduced in order to implement the Second Company Law Directive[1]. This should allow scope to argue that a more purposive interpretation should be given to s 80 in line with the objectives of the Directive. It is clear that the standard form of words used in these resolutions does not offend against the purposes of the Directive. It should therefore be regarded as compliant.

1 Directive 77/91.

2.20 Section 80 authorities may be renewed on an unlimited number of occasions by the general meeting. Any resolution for renewal is subject to the same requirements as the original resolution for authority[1]. Section 80 authorities may also be revoked or varied by the company in general meeting before the date on which they would otherwise have expired[2].

1 CA 1985, s 80(5).
2 CA 1985, s 80(4).

Allotment after expiration of authority

2.21 It is possible for an allotment to be made after the authority has expired, provided that the allotment is made in pursuance of an offer or agreement made by the company before the date of expiry, and that the authority allowed the making of an offer or agreement which would or might require relevant securities to be allotted after the date of expiry. This possibility raises a further point for consideration when drafting a resolution giving s 80 authority. The presumption clearly is that relevant securities may not validly be allotted after the date of expiry, even if the offer or agreement is entered into before the date of expiry. Thus, those concerned with an allotment need to check carefully the date at which the allotment is made as well as the date on when the offer is made or the agreement is entered into. Alternatively, it is necessary to attend to the problem, in advance by drafting the resolution so as to make clear that it is intended to confer authority to allot even after expiry.

2.22 Resolutions under CA 1985, s 80 (including those renewing, varying or revoking authority to allot) are ordinary resolutions, even if their effect is to alter the company's articles[1], but if they are passed as ordinary resolutions they are required to be forwarded to the Registrar within 15 days of being passed[2].

1 CA 1985, s 80(7).
2 CA 1985, s 80(7).

2.23 An allotment made in violation of these rules remains valid[1], but any director who is knowingly a party to the wrongful allotment is guilty of an offence[2]. This last provision may be thought to remove much of the force from the general effect of CA 1985, s 80, for the prospect of prosecution under the section must be remote. In practice the major force of s 80(9) appears to derive from the fact that in many allotments of shares done by private companies professional advisers are involved. These advisers will naturally not be prepared to see their clients commit a criminal offence through oversight (and will not wish to become implicated in any such offence) and will therefore insist on the taking of the necessary steps to regularise the position.

1 CA 1985, s 80(10).
2 CA 1985, s 80(9).

2.24 Section 80(11) of the CA 1985 provides a further exemption from the general provisions of s 80. The section does not apply to any allotment of relevant securities by a company other than a public company originally registered as such if made in pursuance of an offer or agreement made before the date of the holding of the first meeting of the company after its registration or re-registration as a public company[1]. This subsection is relevant in two situations. First, it allows a private company to make an offer or agreement for allotment without complying with s 80 up until the date of its first AGM. Second, a private company which re-registers as public retains the same exemption until the date of its first exemption after re-registration.

1 The section gives an alternative date of 22 June 1982, but this is now obviously obsolete.

Elective regime and section 80

2.25 Section 80A, inserted into the CA 1985 by the Companies Act 1989, deals with the position where a private company has adopted the elective regime for the conduct of its affairs[1]. In the particular context of s 80 the major problem is that the absence of an AGM removes the occasion for passing a s 80 resolution as well as that for regular review of that authority. Section 80A(1) of the CA 1985 allows a company to decide by elective resolution that s 80A shall apply instead of s 80(4), (5). Where this has been done, an authority to allot may be given for a fixed period (not limited to five years) in which case it must state the date on which it is to expire or it may be given for an indefinite period[2]. An authority given for a fixed period may be renewed or further renewed by the company in general meeting[3], whilst any authority given for the purposes of s 80A may be revoked or varied by the company in general meeting[4].

1 For the elective regime generally see CA 1985, ss 80A, 366A, 379A, 381A-381C, 382A-382B, 385A.
2 CA 1985, s 80A(2).
3 CA 1985, s 80A(4).
4 CA 1985, s 80A(3).

2.26 Where an election to apply CA 1985, s 80A ceases to have effect and there is at that time in force an authority for an indefinite period or for more than five years, then the Act presumes that the authority was originally given for a period of five years[1]. Thus, if the authority was given more than five years before the date on which the section 80A election ceases to have effect, the authority is immediately at an end; otherwise it will expire five years after the date on which it was given.

1 CA 1985, s 80A(7).

Pre-emption rights

2.27 Prior to the Companies Act 1980 there was no general rule that existing shareholders were to have any preferential claim on the issue of new shares, nor that on an issue of shares all shareholders (or even all shareholders of a particular class) were to be treated equally[1]. The position was radically altered by the provisions which are now ss 89 ff of the CA 1985, introduced in response to the Second Company Law Directive.

1 *Mutual Life Insurance Co of New York v Rank Organisation Ltd* [1985] BCLC 11 ChD.

2.28 A company proposing to allot equity securities[1] must not allot any of them on any terms to a person unless it has made an offer to each person who holds relevant shares or relevant employee shares to allot to him on the same or more favourable terms a proportion of those securities which is as nearly as practicable equal to the proportion in nominal value held by him of the aggregate of relevant shares and relevant employee shares. A company must not allot any of those securities to a person unless the period during which any such offer may be accepted has expired or the company has received notice of the acceptance or refusal of every offer so made[2]. Thus, existing shareholders are entitled to be offered the new shares pro rata to their existing holdings. This gives them the opportunity to preserve their proportion of the company's shares by taking up the offer. The rule is intended to operate as a check on the power of directors to alter the balance of power within the company by allotting new shares to their own associates.

1 Defined in CA 1985, s 94.
2 CA 1985, s 89(1).

2.29 If any provision of a company's memorandum or articles requires the company, when proposing to allot equity securities consisting of relevant shares of any particular class, not to allot those securities on any terms unless it has complied with the condition that it makes such an offer as is described in CA 1985, s 89(1) to each person who holds relevant shares or relevant employee shares of that class, then subsection (1) does not apply to the allotment of those securities to such a holder or to anyone in whose favour he has renounced his right to their allotment[1].

1 CA 1985, s 89(2) and (3).

2.30 Section 89(1) of the CA 1985 does not apply to a particular allotment of equity securities if these are, or are to be, wholly or partly paid up otherwise than in cash[1]. This is a significant loophole in the protection afforded by s 89, since it allows the directors to circumvent the operation of that section by including a purely nominal non-cash element in the consideration for the shares. The point is less significant in the case of a public company, where the rules in the CA 1985, ss 103 ff would require the non-cash consideration to be valued, a prospect which might discourage the directors from unjustified use of this device. In a private company these rules do not apply. Of course, it remains the duty of the directors to act in the best interests of the company, and an allotment for non-cash consideration might be open to challenge if it could be shown to have been made for an improper purpose[2].

1 CA 1985, s 89(4).
2 See para **2.90** below.

2.31 Securities which a company has offered to allot to a holder of relevant shares or relevant employee shares may be allotted to him, or anyone in whose favour he has renounced his right to their allotment, without contravening CA 1985, s 89(1)(b)[1].

1 CA 1985, s 89(4).

2.32 Section 89(1) of the CA 1985, does not apply to the allotment of securities which would, apart from a renunciation or assignment of the right to their allotment, be held under an employees' share scheme[1].

1 CA 1985, s 89(5).

Section 90 has rules as to the communication of pre-emption offers to shareholders

2.33 An offer shall be in writing and shall be made to a holder of shares either personally or by sending it by post (that is to say, prepaying and posting a letter containing the offer) to him or to his registered address or, if he has no registered address in the United Kingdom, to the address in the United Kingdom supplied by him to the company for the giving of notice to him[1]. If sent by post, the offer is deemed to be made at the time at which the letter would be delivered in the ordinary course of post.

1 CA 1985, s 90(2).

2.34 Where shares are held by two or more persons jointly, the offer may be made to the joint holder first named in the register of members in respect of the shares[1].

1 CA 1985, s 90(3).

2.35 In the case of a holder's death or bankruptcy, the offer may be made:

(a) by sending it by post in a prepaid letter addressed to the persons claiming to be entitled to the shares in consequence of the death or bankruptcy by name, or by the title of representatives of the deceased, or trustee of the bankrupt, or by any like description, at the address in the United Kingdom supplied for the purpose by those so claiming; or

(b) (until such an address has been so supplied) by giving the notice in any manner in which it might have been given if the death or bankruptcy had not occurred[1].

1 CA 1985, s 90(4).

2.36 If the holder has no registered address in the United Kingdom and has not given to the company an address in the United Kingdom for the service of notices on him, or is the holder of a share warrant, the offer may be made by causing it, or a notice specifying where a copy of it can be obtained or inspected, to be published in the Gazette[1].

1 CA 1985, s 90(5).

2.37 The offer must state a period of not less than 21 days during which it may be accepted, and the offer cannot be withdrawn before the end of that period[1].

1 CA 1985, s 90(6).

2.38 Section 90 of the CA 1985 does not invalidate a provision to which s 89(3) applies by reason that that provision requires or authorises an offer under it to be made in contravention of any of s 90(1)–(6), but, to the extent that the provision requires or authorises such an offer to be so made, it is of no effect. Thus, in such a case the requirement to make an offer would remain, but the offer would have to be made in accordance with s 90, whatever the terms of the articles might say.

2.39 Section 91 of the CA 1985 allows a private company to exclude sections 89 and 90 from applying to allotments by a private company of equity securities or to such allotments of a particular description. This may be done by a provision contained in the memorandum or articles of that company.

2.40 A requirement or authority contained in the memorandum or articles of a private company, if it is inconsistent with s 89 or 90, has effect as a provision excluding that subsection; but a provision to which s 89(3) applies is not to be treated as inconsistent with s 89(1).

Section 92 explains the consequences of contravening sections 89 and 90

2.41 If there is a contravention of CA 1985, s 89(1), or of s 90(1)–(5) or s 90(6), or of a provision to which s 89(3) applies, the company, and every officer of it who knowingly authorised or permitted the contravention, are jointly and severally liable to compensate any person to whom an offer should have been made under the subsection or provision contravened for any loss, damage, costs or expenses which the person has sustained or incurred by reason of the contravention.

2.42 However, no proceedings to recover any such loss, damage, costs or expenses shall be commenced after the expiration of two years from the delivery to the Registrar of Companies of the return of allotments in question or, where equity securities other than shares are granted, from the date of the grant.

2.43 It is sometimes said that if an allotment is made in violation of these rules the company is liable to compensate anyone who suffers loss as a result, but no offence is committed, and it appears that those who have been deprived of shares have no right to claim them from the allottees. However, in *Re Thundercrest Ltd*[1] an allotment in breach of these rules was set aside. This case needs to be treated with some caution. The allotment was to the directors themselves, and there was no difficulty about identifying the shares which had been wrongly allotted. The judge accepted that the position would have been much more difficult if these conditions had not been met. The problem to which this decision gives rise is that of understanding whether the setting aside was something to which the applicants were entitled as of right or something which lay in the discretion of the court. In the former, then it is impossible to understand how the rule could operate where the allotment was to outsiders or if the shares had been partly passed on to third parties. If the latter, then it is necessary to ask where this discretion comes from. Certainly there is nothing in CA 1985, s 92 which would support the idea of a discretion. It might be argued (though this does not appear to be the basis of the actual decision) that there was discretion to set the allotment aside as not having been made in the best interests of the company. However, such a solution would merely cause more problems, since it turns attention away from the non-compliance with CA 1985, s 89 and towards the substantive question of fairness. It would therefore not help in cases where the allotment did not appear substantively unfair. The conclusion must be that the decision in *Re Thundercrest* is open to the gravest doubts.

1 [1995] 1 BCLC 117 (Judge Paul Baker QC).

2.44 Sections 89–92 of the CA 1985 are without prejudice to any enactment by virtue of which a company is prohibited (whether generally or in specified circumstances) from offering or allotting equity securities to any person.

2.45 Where a company cannot by virtue of such an enactment offer or allot equity securities to a holder of relevant shares or relevant employee shares, those sections have effect as if the shares held by that holder were not relevant shares or relevant employee shares.

Restrictions on public offer by private company

2.46 Section 81 of the CA 1985 prohibits a private limited company (other than one limited by guarantee and not having a share capital) from offering to the public any shares in or debentures of the company[1]. There is also a prohibition on allotting or agreeing to allot any shares or debentures of the company with a view to any or all of them being offered for sale to the public[2]. The notion of an offer for sale to the public is defined in ss 58–60 of the CA 1985. These provisions were repealed by s 213 of the Financial Services Act 1986 with effect from a series of dates between 1987 and 1995, but with savings for specified purposes, one of which is the incorporation of this definition for the purposes of CA 1985, s 81[3].

1 CA 1985, s 81(1)(a).
2 CA 1985, s 81(1)(b).
3 See SI 1995/1538.

2.47 Section 59(1) of the CA 1985 provides that an offer to the public is to be read as including an offer to any section of the public, whether selected as members or debenture holders of the company concerned, or as clients of the person issuing the prospectus or in any other manner. To this extent the rule may be regarded as very unsatisfactory, since it apparently treats an offer made to the existing shareholders (and not to anyone else) as an offer made to the public.

2.48 Section 60 of the CA 1985 goes onto provide further guidance as to the meaning of 'offer to the public'. Section 60(1) provides that s 59 does not require an offer or invitation to be treated as being made to the public if it can properly be regarded in all the circumstances as not being calculated to result in the shares or debentures becoming available to persons other than those receiving o the offer or invitation. Similarly the offer is not to be regarded as made to the public if it can properly be regarded as a 'domestic concern' of those receiving and making it.

2.49 These provisions are confusing, to put it mildly. It is possible to discern the intention behind them, namely that shares in private companies should not be offered to the world at large. However, two major problems arise, one of definition and one of principle. The definitional question is that already alluded to, namely what is 'the public' for these purposes. The question of principle is whether the intention behind CA 1985, s 81 is still justifiable at all.

Justification of section 81

2.50 Before 1980 it was a requirement for the status of a private company that the articles must contain a share transfer restriction and that there must be no more than 50 members. Thus, the law had a relatively clear notion of what it meant by a private company. Both those requirements were abolished in 1980 (though of course there must still be many companies formed under the old law, whose articles still contain those restrictions. Given the absence of those requirements, it is not at all obvious why private companies should now be prohibited from offering their shares more widely. It is no doubt true that relatively few would wish to do so, but that is no reason to deny the opportunity to those private companies which might on occasion find it helpful. Be that as it may, the restriction remains in force.

Meaning of 'the public'

2.51 In trying to make some sense of ss 59 and 60 of the CA 1985 it should first be understood that s 59(1) does not provide a definition of 'the public' or 'offer to the public'. It merely declares that certain things are to be included within offer to the public. Section 60 of the CA 1985 then removes from the definition some things which would otherwise be within it. What is confusing and puzzling is that some things which would almost certainly not fall within the definition but for s 59(1) are then promptly removed from it by s 60 This observation applies in particular to the case of offers made solely to existing members of the company. Section 59(1) provides that there is an offer to the public where the recipients are selected as members of the company, but s 60 disapplies this where the offer is not likely to lead to the shares being made available more widely than this. This is a requirement which will surely be satisfied in the vast majority of cases where the offer is made only to existing members.

2.52 The only exception would appear to be where the offer is made to existing members with the specific contemplation that the offer will come to the attention of a broader constituency[1]. Such a case would surely in any event fall within the terms of an unglossed prohibition on offers to the public, since it would clearly be intended that at least some shares should be sold to the public. In any event none of this resolves the basic dilemma of deciding who are 'the public' for these purposes. On the one hand it surely cannot be intended to restrict the offering of shares to existing members, since that would make it more or less impossible to bring in any new shareholders. On the other hand the intention of CA 1985, s 81 is presumably to prevent the making of offers to the world at large. The difficulty is to know where the line is to be drawn between these two extremes. It might well be thought that this difficulty reinforces the suggestion made in the previous paragraph that it would be better to repeal s 81 entirely and leave private companies free to offer their shares as they see fit.

1 It is not material that it is intended that the members shall subsequently sell their shares to others.

2.53 Sections 82–87 of the CA 1985 lay down further rules relevant to the issue of shares by means of prospectuses or offers to the public. These rules are of course relevant only to public companies, since private companies are forbidden to issue shares by this means. Sections 81–83, 86 and 87 were repealed from 16 February by the Financial Services Act 1986, s 212(3) and Sch 17, Pt I, to the extent that they would apply to any investment which is subject to a listing application under part IV of the Financial Services Act 1986 (ie investments listed or to be listed on the stock exchange).

2.54 By s 82(1) of the CA 1985 no allotment may be made of a company's shares or debentures in pursuance of a prospectus issued generally, and no proceedings shall be taken on applications made in pursuance of a prospectus so issued, until the beginning of the third day after than on which the prospectus is first so issued or such later time (if any) as may be specified in the prospectus. The beginning of that third day, or that later time, is 'the time of the opening of the subscription lists'.

2.55 In s 82(1) of the CA 1985, the reference to the day on which the prospectus is first issued generally is to the day when it is first so issued as a newspaper advertisement; and if it is not so issued as a newspaper advertisement before the third day after that on which it is first so issued in any other manner, the reference is to the day on which it is first so issued in any manner[1].

1 CA 1985, s 82(3).

2.56 In reckoning for this purpose the third day after another day:

(a) any intervening day which is a Saturday or Sunday, or is a bank holiday in any part of Great Britain, is to be disregarded; and

(b) if the third day (as so reckoned) is itself a Saturday or Sunday, or a bank holiday;

there is to be substituted the first day after that which is none of them[1].

1 CA 1985, s 82(4).

2.57 The validity of an allotment is not affected by any contravention of CA 1985, s 82(1)–(4); but in the event of contravention, the company and every officer of it who is in default is liable to a fine[1].

1 CA 1985, s 82(5).

2.58 As applying to a prospectus offering shares or debentures for sale, the above provisions are modified as follows:

(a) for references to allotment, substitute references to sale; and

(b) for the reference to the company and every officer of it who is in default;

substitute a reference to any person by or through whom the offer is made and who knowingly and wilfully authorises or permits the contravention[1].

1 CA 1985, s 82(6).

2.59 An application for shares in or debentures of a company which is made in pursuance of a prospectus issued generally is not revocable until after the expiration of the third day after the time of the opening of the subscription lists, or the giving before the expiration of that day of the appropriate public notice; and that notice is one given by some person responsible under ss 67–69 for the prospectus and having the effect under those sections of excluding or limiting the responsibility of the giver[1].

1 CA 1985, s 82(7).

2.60 Section 83 of the CA 1985 imposes requirements as to the minimum subscription to be received in relation to a public allotment. No allotment may be made of any share capital of a company offered to the public for subscription unless:

(a) there has been subscribed the amount stated in the prospectus as the minimum amount which, in the opinion of the directors, must be raised by the issue of share capital in order to provide for the matters specified in paragraph 2 of Schedule 3 (preliminary expenses, purchase of property, working capital, etc); and

(b) the sum payable on application for the amount so stated has been paid to and[1] for the purposes of s 83(1)(b), a sum is deemed paid to the company, and received by it, if a cheque for that sum has been received in good faith by the company and the directors have no reason for suspecting that the cheque will not be paid[2].

1 CA 1985, s 83(1).
2 CA 1985, s 83(2).

2.61 The amount so stated in the prospectus is to be reckoned exclusively of any amount payable otherwise than in cash and is known as 'the minimum subscription'[1].

1 CA 1985, s 83(3).

2.62 If the above conditions have not been complied with on the expiration of 40 days after the first issue of the prospectus, all money received from applicants for shares shall be forthwith repaid to them without interest[1].

1 CA 1985, s 83(4).

2.63 If any of the money is not repaid within 48 days after the issue of the prospectus, the directors of the company are jointly and severally liable to repay it with interest at the rate of 5% per annum from the expiration of the 48th day; except that a director is not so liable if he proves that the default in the repayment of the money was not due to any misconduct or negligence on his part[1].

1 CA 1985, s 83(5).

2.64 Any condition requiring or binding an applicant for shares to waive compliance with any requirement of this section is void[1].

1 CA 1985, s 83(6).

2.65 Section 83 of the CA 1985 does not apply to an allotment of shares subsequent to the first allotment of shares offered to the public for subscription[1]. This is an important limit on the section, since it excludes all but the initial placing of shares with the public. It is to be noted that s 84, which is dealt with next, and which also contains rules about allotments to the public, is not limited in this way.

1 CA 1985, s 83(7).

2.66 Section 84(1) of the CA 1985 provides that no allotment shall be made of any share capital of a public company offered for subscription unless:

(a) that capital is subscribed for in full; or

(b) the offer states that, even if the capital is not subscribed for in full, the amount of that capital subscribed for may be allotted in any event or in the event of the conditions specified in the offer being satisfied;

and, where conditions are so specified, no allotment of the capital shall be made by virtue of paragraph (b) unless those conditions are satisfied.

2.67 If shares are prohibited from being allotted by s 84(1) and 40 days have elapsed after the first issue of the prospectus, all money received from applicants for shares shall be forthwith repaid to them without interest[1].

1 CA 1985, s 84(2).

2.68 If any of the money is not repaid within 48 days after the issue of the prospectus, the directors of the company are jointly and severally liable to repay it with interest at the rate of 5% per annum from the expiration of the 48th day; except that a director is not so liable if he proves that the default in repayment was not due to any misconduct or negligence on his part[1].

1 CA 1985, s 84(3).

2.69 Section 84 of the CA 1985 applies in the case of shares offered as wholly or partly payable otherwise than in cash as it applies in the case of shares offered for subscription (the word 'subscribed' in subsection (1) being construed accordingly)[1].

1 CA 1985, s 84(4).

2.70 In s 84(2)(3) of the CA 1985 as they apply to the case of shares offered as wholly or partly payable otherwise than in cash, references to the repayment of money received from applicants for shares include:

(a) the return of any other consideration so received (including, if the case so requires, the release of the applicant from any undertaking); or

(b) if it is not reasonably practicable to return the consideration, the payment of money equal to its value at the time it was so received,

and references to interest apply accordingly[1].

1 CA 1985, s 84(5).

2.71 Any condition requiring or binding an applicant for shares to waive compliance with any requirement of this section is void[1].

1 CA 1985, s 84(6).

2.72 An allotment made by a company to an applicant in contravention of CA 1985, ss 83 or 84 is voidable at the instance of the applicant within one month after the date of the allotment, and not later, and is so voidable notwithstanding that the company is in the course of being wound up[1].

1 CA 1985, s 85.

2.73 If a director of a company knowingly contravenes, or permits or authorises the contravention of, any provision of either of those sections with respect to allotment, he is liable to compensate the company and the allottee respectively for any loss, damages or costs which the company or the allottee may have sustained or incurred by the contravention. However, proceedings to recover any such loss, damages or costs shall not be commenced after the expiration of two years from the date of the allotment.

2.74 The following applies where a prospectus, whether issued generally or not, states that application has been, or will be made, for permission for the shares or debentures offered by it to be listed on any stock exchange.

2.75 An allotment made on an application in pursuance of the prospectus is, whenever made, void if the permission has not been applied for before the third day after the first issue of the prospectus or, if the permission has been refused, before the expiration of three weeks from the date of the closing of the subscription lists or such longer period (not exceeding six weeks) as may, within those three weeks, be notified to the applicant for permission by or on behalf of the stock exchange.

2.76 In reckoning for this purpose the third day after another day:

(a) any intervening day which is a Saturday or Sunday, or is a bank holiday in any part of Great Britain, is to be disregarded; and

(b) if the third day (as so reckoned) is itself a Saturday or Sunday, or a bank holiday, there is to be substituted the first day after that which is none of them.

2.77 Where permission has not been applied for as above, or has been refused as above, the company shall forthwith repay (without interest) all money received from applicants in pursuance of the prospectus.

2.78 If any of the money is not repaid within eight days after the company becomes liable to repay it, the directors of the company are jointly and severally liable to repay the money with interest at the rate of 5% per annum from the expiration of the eighth day, except that a director is not liable if he proves that the default in the repayment of the money was not due to any misconduct or negligence on his part.

2.79 All money received from applicants in pursuance of the prospectus shall be kept in a separate bank account so long as the company may become liable to repay it under subsection (4); and if default is made in complying with this subsection, the company and every officer of it who is in default is liable to a fine.

2.80 Any condition requiring or binding an applicant for shares or debentures to waive compliance with any requirement of this section is void.

2.81 For purposes of this section, permission is not deemed to be refused if it is intimated that the application for it, though not at present granted, will be given further consideration.

2.82 This section has effect in relation to shares or debentures agreed to be taken by a person underwriting an offer of them by a prospectus as if he had applied for them in pursuance of the prospectus.

2.83 The following has effect as regards the operation of CA 1985, s 86 in relation to a prospectus offering shares for sale. Subsections (1) and (2) of that section apply, but with the substitution for the reference in subsection (2) to allotment of a reference to sale. Subsections (4) and (5) of that section do not apply, but:

(a) if the permission referred to in CA 1985, s 86(2) has not been applied for as there mentioned, or has been refused as there mentioned, the offeror of the shares shall forthwith repay (without interest) all money received from applicants in pursuance of the prospectus, and

(b) if any such money is not repaid within eight days after the offeror becomes liable to repay it, he becomes liable to pay interest on the money due, at the rate of 5% per annum from the end of the eighth day.

Subsections (6)–(9) apply, except that in subsection (6):

(a) for the first reference to the company there is substituted a reference to the offeror, and

(b) for the reference to the company and every officer of the company who is in default there is substituted a reference to any person by or through whom the offer is made and who knowingly and wilfully authorises or permits the default.

2.84 Section 88 of the CA 1985 applies to a company limited by shares and to a company limited by guarantee and having a share capital.

2.85 When such a company makes an allotment of its shares, the company shall within one month thereafter deliver to the Registrar of Companies for registration:

(a) a return of the allotments (in the prescribed form) stating the number and nominal amount of the shares comprised in the allotment, the names and addresses of the allottees, and the amount (if any) paid or due and payable on each share, whether on account of the nominal value of the share or by way of premium; and

(b) in the case of shares allotted as fully or partly paid-up otherwise than in cash:

    (i) a contract in writing constituting the title of the allottee to the allotment together with any contract of sale, or for services or other consideration in respect of which that allotment was made (such contracts being duly stamped), and
    (ii) a return stating the number and nominal amount of shares so allotted,

the extent to which they are to be treated as paid-up, and the consideration for which they have been allotted.

2.86 Where such a contract as above mentioned is not reduced to writing, the company shall, within one month after the allotment has been made, deliver to the Registrar of Companies for registration, the prescribed particulars of the contract stamped with the same stamp duty as would have been payable if the contract had been reduced to writing.

2.87 Those particulars are deemed an instrument within the meaning of the Stamp Act 1891; and the Registrar may, as a condition of filing the particulars, require that the duty payable on them be adjudicated under s 12 of that Act.

2.88 If default is made in complying with this section, every officer of the company who is in default is liable to a fine and, for continued contravention, to a daily default fine, but subject as follows.

2.89 In the case of default in delivering to the Registrar within one month after the allotment any document required by this section to be delivered, the company, or any officer liable for the default, may apply to the court for relief; and the court, if satisfied that the omission to deliver the document was accidental or due to inadvertence, or that it is just and equitable to grant relief, may make an order extending the time for the delivery of the document for such period as the court thinks proper.

Issues for improper purposes

2.90 Even where all the statutory procedures have been complied with, it is still necessary for the directors to satisfy themselves that the issue of shares is made for a proper purpose. It must not be forgotten that the power to issue shares is a fiduciary power of the directors and as such must be exercised bona fide and in the best interests of the company. The effect of this principle was considered in two important cases. In *Bamford v Bamford*[1] it was held that an issue of shares which is voidable because the directors were actuated by improper motives and so guilty of misfeasance, can be ratified after full and frank disclosure by the directors to the shareholders by an ordinary resolution of the shareholders in general meeting, though the ordinary resolution ratifying such an issue of shares is not itself an issue of the shares.

1 [1970] Ch 212, [1969] 1 All ER 969, CA.

2.91 In *Hogg v Cramphorn Ltd*[1] the directors had entered into a scheme for issuing shares in order to prevent control of the company from falling into the hands of someone whom they regarded as undesirable in that context. Some shareholders sought to challenge this exercise by the directors of their powers. It was held that the directors had exercised their powers improperly, so that the allotment was liable to be set aside. Nevertheless a majority of the shareholders in general meeting would have power to ratify the issue of the shares, and, accordingly, opportunity should be given for the shareholders in general meeting (at which no votes would be cast in respect of the disputed shares) to decide whether or not to ratify the issue of the shares.

1 [1967] Ch 254, [1966] 3 All ER 420, ChD.

Bonus shares

2.92 Bonus shares are not specifically regulated by the Companies Acts. They arise when a company seeks to reward shareholders by giving them extra shares in the company. This is often done as a bonus for shareholder loyalty. The important point in relation to bonus shares is that CA 1985, s 100 (prohibition of allotment of shares at a discount) must still be complied, as must CA 1985, s 99 (general rules as to payment for shares on allotment). However, s 99(4) expressly preserves the power of a company to allot bonus shares to its members out of sums available for the purpose. In order to prevent infringement of the capital maintenance doctrine these sums must take the form of distributable profits[1].

1 As defined in CA 1985, s 263.

Shares by way of dividend

2.93 It is possible for a company to issue all or part of its dividend in the form of shares in the company. The Companies Acts do not forbid this practice, nor do they contain any provisions regulating the way in which it is done. It is usual for a company wishing to issue dividend shares to offer shareholders the option to take dividends in the form of shares. Some provision must obviously be made for valuing the shares so as to decide how many shares will be issued in lieu of a particular dividend. In quoted companies it is usual to take the market price on the day when the dividend is to be paid. In unquoted companies the directors may set a price when making the offer to shareholders. Shareholders who choose to accept the dividend shares are still deemed for tax purposes to have received the cash equivalent.

Scrip issues

2.94 Scrip issues arise where a company wishes to subdivide its existing share capital into a larger number of shares of smaller value. Since this process has no effect on the total capital available to creditors, the Companies Acts do not regulate it beyond providing in CA 1985, s 121 that such a change may be made by ordinary resolution of the company in general meeting, the resolution being filed with the Registrar.

Rights issues

2.95 Rights issues arise where a company wishes to increase its share capital and offers its shares to existing shareholders pro rata to their existing holdings (whether or not the company is at that time subject to the pre-emption provisions of ss 89 ff of the CA 1985).

PAYMENT FOR SHARES

Means of payment

2.96 The general principle is that shares allotted by a company may be paid for in money or money's worth (including goodwill and know-how)[1]. This provision appears to allow considerable scope for abuse, given the obvious difficulties of valuing either goodwill or know-how (and to a lesser extent many other assets) with any accuracy. In the case of a private company there is no general prohibition on accepting payment in kind.

1 CA 1985, s 99(1).

2.97 In *Park Business Interiors Ltd v Park*[1] the company claimed that shares had been allotted to a director for no consideration and without any genuine assessment by the directors of the adequacy of the consideration. It appeared that the allotment was intended to pay off debts which the director had incurred in setting up the company. The return stated that the shares had been allotted to P as fully paid-up otherwise than in cash and that the consideration was 'debts due by the Company to the allottee'. It was held that the directors of a company are entitled to allot shares for a consideration other than cash and the court would not investigate the adequacy of that consideration unless it was obviously inadequate. A company could agree to reimburse promoters for expenses incurred in preparations for its business and there is no rule that past services to the company could not constitute adequate consideration for the allotment of shares. On the facts the company had, despite the absence of any formal minute, openly agreed to accept liability for P's expenditure and there was nothing to suggest that P and his co-director had failed to adequately consider the sufficiency of the consideration.

1 [1992] BCLC 1034, Ct of Sess (Outer House).

2.98 However, a public company may not accept in payment for its shares an undertaking by which any person will do work for the company or for any other person[1]. It is this rule which gives rise to the difficulties arising under CA 1985, s 45(3), (4), discussed earlier. If a public company does accept such an undertaking, then the holder of the shares at the time when the are treated as paid up is liable to pay to the company the cash equivalent (plus interest[2]) of the amount treated as paid-up in return for the undertaking[3]. In other words the undertaking is not effective to discharge the liability to pay for the shares. The person who becomes liable under this provision is the person who holds the shares[4] at the time when the shares are treated as paid-up. This need not be the original allottee. If, for example, the shares are allotted nil paid, but are then sold by the original allottee, and the company later accepts an undertaking from a subsequent holder in substitution for cash, then it is the subsequent holder who is liable to pay the cash equivalent. This is entirely logical, since the subsequent holder would have been liable in the absence of the undertaking, and the purpose of the provision is to deprive the undertaking of any legal effect.

1 CA 1985, s 99(2).
2 CA 1985, s 99(3)(b).
3 CA 1985, s 99(3).
4 This includes anyone who has an unconditional right to be included in the company's register in respect of those shares or to have an instrument of transfer executed in his favour; CA 1985, s 99(5). Thus it appears that more than one person could be simultaneously liable in respect of the same shares.

2.99 However, s 99(4) of the CA 1985 goes on to provide that s 99 does not affect the power of a company to issue bonus shares and to apply money available for the purpose (ie distributable profits) in paying up those shares.

2.100 Section 100 of the CA 1985 prohibits the allotment of shares at a discount. Section 100(2) makes the discount ineffective by providing that the allottee remains liable to pay to the company the amount of the discount, plus interest.

2.101 Some explanation is required of the relationship between the CA 1985, ss 97 and 98 (commissions), and ss 99 and 100. Section 100, in referring to a discount, is understood as referring to the situation where the company seeks to issue shares for less than their *nominal* value. This is a practice which, if allowed, would obviously undermine the capital maintenance doctrine. However, it is also a practice which is easily avoided, since, apart from this section, there is no necessary relationship between the nominal value of the shares and the price at which they are allotted.

2.102 At the present day it is common to find listed companies whose shares have a very low nominal value[1] but a much higher issue price. The importance of CA 1985, s 100 is therefore very limited. The word 'discount' as used in s 98 can be seen to have a different meaning from the same word as used in s 100. Section 98 is really intended to deal with what would normally be called 'commission' and merely uses the word 'discount' in order to catch an alternative way of presenting what is in substance a commission.

1 For example Abbey National plc has 10p shares, which were allotted in 1989 for £1.30; BT has 25p shares, which were allotted at various times in the early 1990's for prices up to £4.15.

2.103 Section 102 of the CA 1985 imposes restrictions on the acceptance of long-term undertakings as payment for shares. It applies only to public companies, which are forbidden to allot shares in return for a consideration which consists of or includes an undertaking which is to be or may be performed more than five years after the date of the allotment. This rule should firstly be understood in conjunction with the rule in CA 1985, s 99(2)[1] prohibiting the acceptance of an undertaking to do work or perform services. Section 99(2) is wider than section 102 in that it applies to acceptance of payment for shares *at any time* whereas section 102 applies only to the initial allotment. Thus s 99(2) would apply where shares have been allotted partly paid and the company proposes to accept an undertaking to do work in full or part payment of a call on the shares. At the same time s 99(2) is narrower than s 102 in that it applies only to undertakings to do work or perform services, whereas s 102 applies to any kind of undertaking. Where an allotment is made in contravention of s 102(1) the allottee remains liable to the company to make good the shortfall between the amount of cash actually paid (if any) and the full price of the shares[2].

1 See para **2.96** above.
2 CA 1985, s 102(2).

2.104 Section 102(3) of the CA 1985 declares void any variation of the original contract of allotment[1] which would introduce a contravention of s 102(1). This is a simple anti-avoidance provision, designed to prevent the subsequent introduction of improper terms into the contract. Section 102(4) goes on to declare that the principle applies even where the original contract was entered into at a time before the public company re-registered as a public company.

1 Which for these purposes includes an ancillary contract relating to payment for the shares; CA 1985, s 102(7).

2.105 Section 102(5), (6) of the CA 1985 deals with the position where a public company lawfully accepts an undertaking which is to be performed within five years but the undertaking is not in fact so performed. In this event the allottee becomes liable at the end of the five years to pay to the company so much of the purchase price of the shares as was to have been treated as satisfied by performance of the undertaking, plus interest. This is another liability which appears to remain on the allottee, irrespective of the subsequent ownership of the shares.

2.106 Section 103 of the CA 1985 imposes further requirements on a public company which wishes to allot shares as fully or partly paid-up in return for a consideration which is not wholly in cash. The purpose of s 103 is to make it more difficult for public companies to accept a non-cash consideration which is obviously inadequate compared with the notional issue price of the shares. To this end the section requires that the consideration be valued before the allotment is made. Under s 103(1)(a) there must be an independent report as to the value of the consideration for the allotment prepared by a person appointed by the company for that purpose under the procedure laid down in s 108[1] and under s 103(1)(b) that report must have been presented to the company during the six months immediately preceding the date of the allotment. Under s 103(1)(c) a copy of the report must be sent to the proposed allottee before the allotment is made. Section 103 does not apply to amounts allotted to paying up shares from the company's reserve accounts or profit and loss account[2]. This follows the general principle that the valuation and other capital maintenance provisions do not apply to allotments to the extent that they are bonus allotments, since the capital maintenance doctrine is not infringed by capitalising profits of the company.

1 See para **2.127** below.
2 CA 1985, s 103(2).

2.107 Section 103 of the CA 1985 also contains a provision similar to that found in section 44(4). It applies where the allotment of shares is made under an arrangement (including, but not limited to) an arrangement under s 425 of the CA 1985[1] by which the consideration is to be the transfer to the company (or the cancellation) of some or all of the shares of another company. Although this is obviously a case of non-cash consideration, s 103(1) is excluded, provided that participation in the arrangement is open to all the holders of shares (or shares in the affected class of shares) in the other company[2]. Section 103(5) provides a further exception where the allotment of shares is made in connection with its proposed merger with another company.

1 CA 1985, s 103(7).
2 CA 1985, s 103(4).

2.108 Section 103(6) of the CA 1985 deals with the consequences of contraventions of s 103. If a company allots shares when the allottee has not received the valuer's report on the consideration or when there has been some other contravention of s 103 or 108 which the allottee knew or ought to have known amounted to a contravention, then the allottee remains liable to pay the cash equivalent of the amount which was treated as paid-up in return for the non-cash consideration, plus interest. However, non-compliance with s 103 is not a regulatory offence, and no liability therefore attaches to the company or any of its officers. At first sight it may appear odd that the allottee is the only one who suffers. It does appear appropriate to retain the liability upon the allottee, since the major purpose of the section is capital maintenance, and this is achieved by provisions which in effect deem the non-cash consideration to be inadequate if the necessary procedures have not been followed, and therefore insist that the deficiency be made good. At the same time the section gives surprising prominence to the sending of the valuer's report to the allottee. It is not easy to see whom this requirement is meant to protect.

2.109 There are two possible problems arising from the fact that the consideration is something other than cash. The first is that the consideration is too low, whilst the second is that it is too high. If the consideration is too low, then the policy of capital maintenance would suggest that the allottee should remain liable to make good the difference. Whether the consideration is in fact too low might reasonably be determined by the valuation report, accepting the impossibility of achieving exact valuations for many forms of non-cash consideration. However, the liability of the allottee should depend on what is said in the valuation report, not on the purely formalistic question of whether that report has been sent to the allottee at the appropriate time.

2.110 Section 103 of the CA 1985 also makes the allottee liable if there has been some other contravention of the section of which he knew or ought to have known. This too seems to contradict the capital maintenance principle. If the consideration is shown to be inadequate, then the allottee should be liable to make good the difference, irrespective of his state of knowledge. If the breach of s 103 is in some respect which does not go to the adequacy of the consideration, then the imposition of this liability on the allottee appears draconian and disproportionate. At the other end of the spectrum is the case where the non-cash consideration is excessive. In this event it might be suggested that the requirement for the report to be sent to the allottee is intended for the protection of the allottee. Unfortunately, applying this reasoning, the sanction for failure to send the report makes no sense, since the sanction bites only on the allottee. In any event, it seems unlikely that the requirement is there for the benefit of the allottee.

2.111 Moreover, writing the requirement in this way allows the company to obtain an apparent double benefit. If it deliberately fails to send the report, then the allottee is liable to provide the cash consideration as well as the non-cash consideration. It seems harsh that the company should be in a position to benefit in this way from its own possibly deliberate wrongdoing.

2.112 This in turn leads to the consideration of another issue which CA 1985, s 103 does not resolve. Is it in fact correct to say that the allottee remains liable to provide the non-cash consideration as well as the cash consideration? The wording of s 103 clearly imposes liability for the latter, but the section says nothing about the liability for the former. If the company is allowed to claim both, there is an obvious potential for unjust enrichment. This is especially so where the non-cash consideration was in fact adequate, but liability is imposed because of some breach of s 103 (including the failure to send the valuation report, since, as was pointed out above, this is not by itself evidence of the inadequacy of the consideration). Even where the non-cash consideration is somewhat inadequate there is still the potential for unjust enrichment, since the allottee remains liable to pay the full amount which the non-cash consideration was intended to represent, not just the amount by which it is found to be inadequate. It is hard to imagine that a court would be happy with this outcome, but a number of procedural and other difficulties stand in the way of achieving what might be regarded as a just result.

2.113 The first problem arises if the company sues for the cash equivalent after receiving some or all of the value of the non-cash consideration. To allow the action in full obviously produces unjust enrichment, yet the right of recovery is clearly awarded by the statute, which makes no mention of apportionment, nor of any discretion for the court to reduce the amount awarded or to refuse the action entirely. Thus it appears that the action would necessarily succeed.

2.114 However, even if the company has not at the time of the action received any part of the non-cash consideration, there is still the potential for unjust enrichment, since the company's right to obtain the non-cash consideration is not necessarily affected by the exercise of its statutory right. This point is, it must be said, rather less clear. The right to claim the non-cash consideration is presumably contractual and as such subject to normal common law and equitable constraints. It might therefore be possible to argue unjust enrichment as a defence to a subsequent action to recover the non-cash consideration.

2.115 However, it appears that this will to some extent depend on the nature of that consideration. Given that a public company is in any event forbidden to allot shares in return for an undertaking to do work or perform services[1], it would seem that the non-cash consideration is in most cases likely to take the form of some kind of property, often tangible property, though intangibles such as intellectual property rights would also in principle be acceptable. If there is a contract to transfer the property, then the effect is presumably that the company is already in equity the owner of the property and is merely seeking to perfect its legal title. In such a case it is by no means obvious how the standard notions of unjust enrichment can be invoked to provide a defence to the company's claim.

1 CA 1985, s 99(2).

2.116 Of course one obvious and initially attractive answer to this lengthy discussion of the company's remedies would be that in many cases the company would choose not to exercise its rights under CA 1985, s 103 in full, or at all. That is no doubt true, but the statement only serves to raise a number of other difficulties about s 103. Given the perception that the aim of the section is capital maintenance, there might seem to be some oddity in the idea that the company, having discovered from the valuation report that the non-cash consideration is inadequate, should be at liberty nevertheless to accept that consideration in discharge of the liability to pay for the shares and should not be under any obligation to claim the deficiency from the allottee. Yet neither s 103 nor any other provision of the Companies Acts requires it to do so. It is to be supposed that the answer to this point is that the exercise of the company's rights under s 103 is a matter for the discretion of the directors. Like every other power of the directors it must be exercised bona fide and in the best interests of the company. Thus, in the case where the consideration is found to be inadequate, the company ought to bring an action for the cash consideration.

2.117 It would presumably be open to the company to offer to compromise that action on payment of the difference between the actual value of the non-cash consideration and the amount which was treated as paid-up in return for it. Where it appears that the non-cash consideration was in fact adequate, even though the requirements of CA 1985, s 103 were not observed, the directors would presumably be at liberty to take a commercial decision that it would not be in the best interests of the company to seek to assert its statutory rights.

2.118 Section 104 of the CA 1985 deals with transfers to public companies of non-cash assets in what the section calls the 'initial period'. This period is two years from the date on which the company is issued by the Registrar with a certificate under s 117 declaring that it is entitled to do business[1]. During that period the section restricts the company from entering into an agreement for the transfer of one or more non-cash assets to the company. The restrictions are imposed when the proposed transferor is a subscriber to the memorandum of the company (or a member of the company on the date when it is re-registered as a public company[2]) and the consideration which the company proposes to give for the transfer is at least equal in value, at the time of the agreement, to one-tenth of the nominal value of the company's issued share capital at that time[3]. It is important to note the reference here to the *nominal* value of the issued share capital. The section does not say that any premium on the nominal value can be taken into account. Thus, where the company has issued shares for an amount significantly in excess of their nominal value, there is a greatly increased risk that the provisions of this section will apply. On the other hand, the section is restricted to cases where the proposed transferor of the assets is a subscriber of the memorandum. This is a somewhat surprising provision, since it offers ample opportunity to circumvent the section. Given that it is common for companies to be incorporated by company formation agents, in which case the subscribers to the memorandum (who will probably never actually become shareholders) have no long-term connection with the company, it is easy enough to ensure that anyone who proposes to transfer assets to the company within the initial period is not a subscriber to the memorandum. Of course the directors will still need to consider whether the proposed transfer is in the company's best interests, but CA 1985, s 104 will have been avoided.

1 CA 1985, s 104(2). For CA 1985, s 117 see Chapter 1.
2 CA 1985, s 104(3).
3 CA 1985, s 104(1).

2.119 Where CA 1985, s 104 applies certain procedures have to be followed before the transfer of the assets is permissible. These are set out in s 104(4):

(a) the consideration to be received by the company (the asset or the value to it of the transfer of the asset to another person[1]) and any non-cash consideration to be given by the company must have been valued under s 109[2];

(b) a report with respect to that consideration must have been made to the company in accordance with that section within the six months immediately preceding the date of the agreement;

(c) the terms of the agreement must have been approved by an ordinary resolution of the company;

(d) not later than the giving of the notice of the meeting at which the resolution is proposed copies of the resolution and the valuation report must have been circulated to the members of the company entitled to receive the notice and to the other party to the proposed agreement, whether or not that person is also a member of the company.

1 CA 1985, s 104(5)(a).
2 See para **2.136** below.

2.120 Section 104 of the CA 1985 does not apply where the company in the ordinary course of its business enters into an agreement for the transfer of an asset of a class which it is part of the company's normal business to acquire[1].

1 CA 1985, s 104(6).

2.121 Section 105 of the CA 1985 deals with the consequences of contravening s 104. Section 105(2) applies where the other party to the transaction has not received the valuer's report required by CA 1985, s 103 or where there has been some other contravention of ss 103, s 108(1)(2) or (5) or s 109, which the other party to the transaction knew or ought to have known amounted to a contravention[1]. In this event the company is entitled to recover from the other person any consideration given by it under the agreement or an amount equal to the value of that consideration at the date of the agreement. The agreement itself becomes void, in so far as not already carried out. These provisions give rise to some, but not all, of the difficulties previously discussed in connection with s 103. This time it is clear that the underlying agreement is prospectively voided, which deals with the case where the asset has not been transferred. However, it does not deal fully with the case where the asset has already been transferred. The logical corollary of saying that the company can get back whatever consideration it has provided ought to be that the asset must be returned to the transferor; yet CA 1985, s 105(2) conspicuously fails to say this. It would be absurd to conclude that the company can keep both the asset and the consideration which it originally gave for it, yet this is the apparent result of the section.

1 CA 1985, s 105(1).

2.122 Another difficulty mentioned in connection with CA 1985, s 103 and which recurs here is that the full set of sanctions is imposed merely for failure to deliver a copy of the report in good time. This makes no more sense here than it did in the context of s 103.

2.123 Section 105(3) of the CA 1985 makes special provision for contraventions of s 104 in the specific case where the agreement for the transfer of the asset included an agreement for the allotment of shares in the company. In this event s 105(2) is disapplied 'in so far as' the agreement is for the allotment of shares. Instead the sanction is the same as that under CA 1985, s 103, namely that the allottee remains liable to pay in cash the value which was to have been treated as paid up by the transfer of the asset. This solution simply takes the case back within the s 103 regime, so that all the problems of that section are again relevant. When s 105(3) used the phrase 'in so far as' the agreement is for the allotment of shares it apparently means that the allotment of shares remains valid, though the allottee is liable to pay for them as just mentioned. What is less clear is what happens in relation to other consideration given by the company. Presumably this remains recoverable under s 105(2) since, to the extent that the company has given any other consideration, the agreement is not one for the allotment of shares and s 105(3) apparently does not apply.

2.124 Finally, in relation to ss 104 and 105 of the CA 1985 it is to be observed that the possibility of the company allotting shares in return for the asset transfer is the most obvious reason why these sections are found in a part of the Act headed 'Amount to be paid for shares: the means of payment'. At the same time it is equally clear that selling an asset to a company at an overvalue is one way in which disguised returns of capital to the shareholders can take place. Sections 104 and 105 do to some extent make this more difficult at least in the initial period of a public company. However, these sections do not apply to private companies, nor do they apply outside the initial period. Even where they do apply, they require only the existence and disclosure of a report. It is still open to the shareholders to approve the transaction even where the report suggests that proper value is not being obtained. This seems odd, given that the capital maintenance doctrine is there for the benefit of creditors rather than for the benefit of shareholders.

2.125 Section 106 of the CA 1985 deals very briefly with a point relating to shares issued to the subscribers of a memorandum of a public company in pursuance of undertakings given by them in the memorandum. It requires, without exception, that these shares must be paid-up in cash. Its importance is of course restricted by the fact that in the memorandum subscribers frequently agree to take only a very small number of shares (sometimes only one) and that in many cases these shares are never in fact allotted.

2.126 Section 107 of the CA 1985 defines the appropriate rate of interest where, under any of ss 99–105 the payment of money by, for example, an allottee of shares is declared to be subject to interest. The rate is 5% per annum or such other rate as may be provided by Statutory Instrument.

Sections 108 to 111 Valuation of shares

2.127 A number of the provisions considered above have required companies to obtain valuations of non-cash consideration in certain circumstances. Sections 108–111 of the CA 1985 set out the detailed provisions for the obtaining of those valuations.

2.128 Section 108 of the CA 1985 applies to valuations which are required under ss 44 or 103. It stipulates that the valuation report must be made by an 'independent person' which s 108(1) defines as meaning a person who is at the time of the report qualified to act as an auditor of the company. In practice it is not uncommon for the company to appoint its auditor to carry out this function, though of course the section does not say that the valuer must be or need ever have been the company's auditor.

2.129 Section 108(2) of the CA 1985 goes on to authorise the valuer to commission or accept a valuation from another person. It must appear to the appointed valuer reasonable to proceed in this way, and the person whose report is commissioned or accepted must be someone who appears to the valuer to have the necessary knowledge and experience to value the consideration[1]. Moreover, that person must not be an officer or servant[2] of the company or of a company in the same group as the company. Nor may he be the partner or employee of an officer or servant of the company. Obviously this provision is inserted to ensure the independence of the person preparing the valuation. Where this approach is adopted, the person so commissioned produces a valuation and a report sufficient to enable the appointed valuer to make his own report to the company.

1 CA 1985, s 108(2)(a).
2 Not for these purposes including an auditor; CA 1985, s 108(3).

2.130 This provision is a curious mixture of the sensible, the formalistic and the obscure. It is obviously sensible that the actual valuation should be carried out by someone who is both independent and competent. There may, for example, be cases where what is required is the valuation of some piece of property, real or personal. This may call for the services of an expert in the particular field, and it is quite likely that a person qualified to act as auditor of the company will not be such an expert. In those circumstances the CA 1985 adopts the curiously formalistic device of requiring the qualified auditor to be appointed as 'valuer' but allowing him to rely on a report from the genuine expert. It is not at all obvious why the Act does not adopt the much simpler solution of allowing the genuine expert to be appointed as valuer in the first place.

2.131 Section 108(4) of the CA 1985 specifies the required content of the valuer's report. It must state:

(a) the nominal value of the shares to be wholly or partly paid for by the consideration in question;

(b) the amount of any premium payable on the shares;

(c) the description of the consideration given for the shares; in respect of the part of the consideration which he has valued, the report must state what that consideration is, the method used to value it and the date of the valuation;

(d) the extent to which the nominal value of the shares and any premium are to be treated as paid up respectively by the consideration and in cash.

2.132 In addition, s 108(5) of the CA 1985 applies where the valuer has taken advantage of the option to have the actual valuation performed by some other person. The report must then state the other person's name and indicate what knowledge and experience he has to carry out the valuation. In respect of the part of the consideration which he has valued, the report must state what that consideration is, the method used to value it and the date of the valuation.

2.133 Section 108(6) of the CA 1985 requires that the valuer's report be accompanied by a note stating the following things:

(a) in the case of a valuation actually performed by some other person that it appeared reasonable to the valuer to arrange for or to accept that valuation;

(b) that the method of valuation was reasonable in all the circumstances (this applies whoever actually makes the valuation);

(c) that it appears to the valuer that there has been no material change in the value of the consideration in question since the valuation;

(d) that on the basis of the valuation the value of the consideration, together with any cash by which the shares are to be paid-up is not less than the amount which is to be treated as paid-up. In other words, the note must state that the company will receive proper value for the shares (to the extent that they are treated as paid-up) if it accepts the consideration offered – cash and non-cash together.

2.134 Section 108(7) of the CA 1985 deals with the relatively unusual situation where the non-cash consideration is to be used partly in payment for the shares and partly for something else. Here the problem is to work out the relative value of the two elements so that it again becomes possible to establish that the company is receiving fair value for the shares. Section 108(7) varies the earlier parts of s 108 by providing that references to the consideration accepted by the company are to be treated as if they were references to the proportion of the consideration which is properly attributable to payment for the shares. The valuer must carry out or arrange for the carrying out of such valuations as will allow him to determine that proportion and his report must state what valuations have been made under section 108(7), together with the reason for, method and date of any such valuation and any other matters which may be relevant to that determination.

2.135 Section 108(7) of the CA 1985 is certainly the least satisfactory part of s 108. The difficulty arising in this situation is that the valuer cannot be satisfied simply to value the consideration which the company is going to receive, Instead, he must look also at the other consideration (ie apart from the shares) which the company is going to provide. Only then can he work out the total value of the consideration which the company will provide and derive from that the proportion which is represented by the value of the shares.

2.136 Section 109 of the CA 1985 makes further provision for the valuation and report required under s 104 where a non-cash asset is transferred to a public company in the initial period of two years from the date of incorporation or of re-registration as a public company. Section 109(2) sets out the requirements for the content of the valuer's report. It must:

(a) state the consideration to be received by the company, describing the asset in question and the consideration to be given by the company, in each case mentioning also any amount to be made up in cash;

(b) state the method and date of valuation;

(c) contain or be accompanied by a note setting out the same matters as are required in the note under s 108, above;

(d) contain or be accompanied by a note that on the basis of the valuation the value of the consideration to be received by the company is not less than the value of the consideration to be given by it.

2.137 Section 109(3) of the CA 1985 then deals with the equivalent of the problem identified in s 108(7), namely the case where consideration given for the transfer of an asset includes consideration given partly for its transfer and partly for something else. In such a case it is necessary to determine what proportion of the total consideration is being given for the asset; to this end the valuer must arrange for any necessary valuations and his report must detail those valuations, indicating who did the valuation, when and on what basis and setting out any other matters which may be relevant in the particular case.

2.138 Section 110 of the CA 1985 is an important section dealing with the rights of a person carrying out a valuation under ss 103 or 104. Section 110(1) confers upon the valuer the right to require from the officers of the company such information and explanation as he thinks necessary to enable him to carry out the valuation and provide the report and note required under ss 108 and 109, as the case may be.

2.139 To reinforce this right, CA 1985, s 110(2) creates a regulatory offence, which is committed by anyone who, in making a statement, oral or written, to a person carrying out a valuation or report under s 108 which purports to convey information to which that person is entitled under s 110(1)[1] and which is knowingly or recklessly misleading, false or deceptive in a material particular. The penalty is a fine or imprisonment or both.

1 CA 1985, s 110(3).

2.140 Section 111 of the CA 1985 deals with matters in connection with reports and valuations which are required to be filed with the Registrar of Companies. Where a company receives a report made under s 108 as to the value of consideration in return for which it proposes to allot shares, a copy of that report must be delivered to the Registrar at the same time as it files the return of the allotment of those shares under s 88[1].

1 CA 1985, s 111(1).

2.141 A company which has passed a resolution under CA 1985, s 104 with respect to the transfer of an asset in return for non-cash consideration during the initial period must within 15 days of the passing of the resolution (not the transfer of the asset) file with the Registrar a copy of the resolution and of the valuer's report required under s 104 and prepared under s 109[1]. Contravening any of these requirements is a regulatory offence. Contravention of s 111(1) imposes liability to a fine, and a daily default fine, on every officer of the company who is in default, though the court has discretion to grant relief against that fine[2]. Contravention of s 111(2) similarly produces a fine and daily default fine for every officer of the company who is in default, but this time there is no discretion to grant relief against that fine.

1 CA 1985, s 111(2).
2 CA 1985, s 111(3).

2.142 At first sight ss 108–111 of the CA 1985, when combined with ss 103 and 104, appear to afford considerable protection against the risk that a company will, either by accident or by design, accept inadequate non-cash consideration in return for shares (and in other broader circumstances in the case of s 104). In fact, closer analysis reveals that the protection given by these provisions is much narrower than that. Where non-cash consideration is being valued for its adequacy in paying for shares, the only question as to which the valuer has to be satisfied is that the non-cash consideration provides adequate value (taking into account any cash element) for the issue price of the shares. However, there is little to stop the company from reducing the issue price of the shares in order to match the value of the consideration as determined by the valuer. Shares may not be issued at less than their nominal value[1], but it was explained earlier that this provides no significant obstacle, since the nominal value can be set very low and the shares issued with a substantial premium.

1 CA 1985, s 98.

2.143 There may be something of a problem where shares are being issued simultaneously to more than one person and it becomes necessary to issue them at a higher price to one than to the other; but even this is not a problem of company law, since it is for the directors to determine the price at which shares are allotted. As ever, the power to issue shares must be exercised bona fide in the best interests of the company, but in any given case the directors might well be able to say that they got the best price they could for the shares (and it might be that this price differed as between two different allottees) and that it was still in the company's best interests to have the new share capital and/or the non-cash asset and/or the particular individuals as shareholders.

2.144 The conclusion to be drawn from this must be that these provisions serve solely to reinforce the capital maintenance doctrine. They do this by ensuring that the amount which is added to the company's share capital as shown in its balance sheet is truly represented by available assets which are worth at least as much as the amount credited in respect of them. They have nothing to do with the prudence of the share allotment in terms of the company's best interests.

Sections 111A-116 Other matters

2.145 These sections deal with a number of miscellaneous matters arising out of allotment, etc. Section 111A, added by the Companies Act 1989, s 131(1) as from 1 April 1990, provides that a person is not debarred from obtaining damages or compensation from a company solely by reason of being or having been a shareholder or having a right to apply or subscribe for shares or to be included in the company's register in respect of shares.

2.146 Section 112 of the CA 1985 deals with the liability of subsequent holders of shares allotted. Section 112(1) applies when shares are allotted in such circumstances that there has been a contravention of ss 99, 100, 101 or 103 and by virtue of that contravention someone (usually the original allottee) is liable under the section contravened to pay some amount of money to the company, or where there has been a contravention of s 102 or a failure to carry out a term of a contract as mentioned in s 102(5) or (6). Section 112(1) lays down the general principle that in such cases a subsequent holder (apparently any subsequent holder, not just the person who bought from the original allottee) is jointly and severally liable to pay the amount which the original allottee would have been liable to pay. The liability thus spreads down the chain of subsequent holders of the shares, all becoming jointly and severally liable to pay the money, subject to possible exemption under s 112(3).

2.147 Section 112(2) of the CA 1985 applies in cases where there has been a contravention of s 104 (transfer of non-cash asset in initial period) and shares allocated in pursuance of an agreement contravening that section are subsequently transferred to another person. Again, the subsequent holder[1] is jointly and severally liable with all the other holders of the shares to pay the amounts due under s 105. This liability is again subject to the possibility of relief under s 112(3).

1 Including anyone who has an unconditional right to be included in the register in respect of those shares or to have an instrument of transfer effected in his favour; CA 1985, s 112(4).

2.148 Section 112(3) of the CA 1985 exempts a subsequent holder of shares from liability under s 112(1) or (2) if he is a purchaser for value and at the time of purchase did not have actual notice of the contravention or if he derived title (directly or indirectly) from a person who became a holder after the date of the contravention and who was not liable under s 112(1) or (2). The practical effect of this is severely to undermine the apparent principle stated in s 112(1), (2). As soon as the shares are transferred to a purchaser for value without actual notice of the contravention, the liability to make good the missing amounts ceases to spread. It cannot then pass to any subsequent holder, regardless of the circumstances of that person's acquisition of the shares or of his state of mind.

2.149 Section 113 of the CA 1985 provides for the possibility of relief from certain liabilities arising under CA 1985, ss 99 ff. This possibility is at the discretion of the court. It arises where a person is liable to a company under any of ss 99, 102, 103, 105, 112 (by reference to a contravention of ss 99 or 103 or 112(2) or (5) in relation to payment for any shares in the company or is liable by virtue of an undertaking given to the company in or in connection with payment for shares. Section 113(1) then allows the person liable to make an application to court for relief from that liability. Section 113(2) then gives the court power to exempt the applicant from liability in respect of the principal sum only if and to the extent that it appears to the court just and equitable to do so having regard to certain specified considerations which are discussed below and in relation to interest on the principal sum only if and to the extent that this appears just and equitable (but without regard to any specific considerations).

2.150 Section 113(3) of the CA 1985 then goes on to list the matters which must be considered in an application for relief from liability in respect of the principal sum. There are three matters listed in s 113(3), as follows:

(a) whether the applicant has paid or is liable to pay any amount in respect of any other liability in connection with those shares, either under the sections mentioned or by virtue of any undertaking given in or in connection with payment for those shares;

(b) whether anyone else has paid or is likely to pay any such amount;

(c) whether the applicant or anyone else has performed or is likely to perform any such undertaking or has done or is likely to do any other thing in payment or part payment for those shares.

2.151 Before considering each of these matters in detail it is appropriate to refer also to CA 1985, s 113(5), which sets out overriding principles which the court must bear in mind in exercising its discretion to grant relief under s 113. There are two of these. The first is a restatement of the importance of the capital maintenance doctrine. The court must remember that a company which has allotted shares should receive money or money's worth at least equal in value to so much of the issue price of the shares as is treated as paid-up in return for that consideration. The second principle is that where the company would, but for the grant of exemption under this section, have more than one remedy against a particular person, it should be for the company to decide which remedy it should remain entitled to pursue.

2.152 The first of these principles may be summarised as meaning that it will almost always be expected that someone will make good any liability resulting from a breach of the sections presently under consideration. Thus there can be little prospect of an order for exemption if the applicant appears to be the only person who can readily be located and who has the resources to make good the deficit. In this sense the first overriding principle may be regarded as logically linked to the second of the three matters mentioned in s 113(3). On the other hand it might be thought that there were quite good grounds for exemption if it appeared in a particular case that despite the technical breach of one of the statutory provisions the company had in fact received full value for the shares allotted. Although this is not one of the matters referred to in s 113(3), adherence to the overriding principles could well be used as a ground for persuading the court to avoid the obviously unjust result which would arise if the company had received full value and then sought to recover the cash equivalent as well. The second overriding principle may be regarded as linked to the first of the matters mentioned in s 113(3). It appears that both are directed to the situation where there has been a breach of more than one of the sections here considered. In a few cases it might be that the amount of the liability would not be the same under each of the sections.

2.153 Section 113 of the CA 1985 then appears to contemplate that an order might be made relieving against some but not all of these liabilities, though the logic if the overriding principle is that the company ought to be able to choose which liability will be left intact. Given that in such a case the company is likely to want to preserve the liability which would allow it the largest recovery, it might be supposed that an applicant should either ask only for the release of the lesser liability or should obtain confirmation from the company of which one it wants to preserve.

2.154 Section 113(4) of the CA 1985 imposes a further restriction on the granting of relief. This has effect where the liability arises by virtue of an undertaking given to the company in or in connection with payment for shares. The court may then grant relief from liability only if and to the extent that it appears just and equitable to do so having regard to whether the applicant has paid or is liable to pay any amount in respect of liability arising in relation to the shares under any of the relevant sections and whether anyone else has paid or is likely to pay such an amount.

2.155 Section 113(6), (7) of the CA 1985 then go on to deal with the possibility of contribution actions in cases where more than one person is liable to make good any deficiency under the sections here considered. Although it is clear that such contribution actions can be brought, s 113(7) gives the court a discretion to apportion the liability among the parties to the claim in accordance with the court's view of their respective culpability in relation to the liability.

2.156 Section 113(8) of the CA 1985 deals only with liability under s 105(2) (liability for non-performance of non-cash obligation on transfer of asset to public company in the initial period). It allows the court to reduce the liability of the applicant to the extent that it appears just and equitable to do so, having regard to anything done by the applicant towards carrying out his obligations.

2.157 Considered as a whole, s 113 of the CA 1985 appears a curious mixture. It represents an uncomfortable attempt at compromise between the principle of capital maintenance and the notion that the liabilities imposed by these sections can cause hardship. A much simpler solution would have been to impose the basic liabilities and then not allow the court any discretion to grant relief from them. Many (admittedly not all) of the difficult situations which can then arise would be dealt with, either on the basis that the company would not think it expedient to bring an action if it had received full value, or on the basis that the company could not in any event recover the same loss twice over. The major difficulty which would have remained under this scheme would have been that caused by the bringing of contribution actions, and that could have been dealt with by leaving the current s 113(7) in place. Instead the legislature has opted for a compromise under which there is an apparently general discretion to relieve against liability, which discretion is then seriously undermined by the imposition of a number of apparently very narrow criteria. At a technical level this is made even worse by the confusion between the two overriding principles and the three matters to which regard is to be had. That is a most unfortunate piece of drafting, but even without it the section would be very difficult to apply.

2.158 The matters mentioned in CA 1985, s 113(3) appear to operate in peculiar ways. The fact that the applicant has some other liability to pay seems an odd point to take into account, given that the only effect of this will be to make him liable under one head rather than another. It seems unlikely that taking this into account will lead to complete exoneration. The fact that someone else has paid the money would lead to the conclusion that the company cannot now sue the applicant anyway (double recovery) so that relief is unnecessary, save to the extent that there might be a contribution action, which is in any event dealt with under s 113(7). The likelihood that someone else will pay is similarly not really a reason for granting relief. Why not wait and see whether that person in fact pays, in which case the matter falls back into the previous category. The same point may be made about the performance of undertakings or the doing of other things promised in return for the shares.

2.159 Moreover, it is not clear whether these are the only matters which can be taken into account under CA 1985, s 113(3), though the wording of s 113(2) rather suggests that they are. If that is so, then the reasonableness of the behaviour of the applicant and the hardship likely to result from the imposition of liability, for example, are not factors which can be taken into account. It is hard to avoid the conclusion that relief under s 113 is only likely to be granted in cases where it is not really needed.

2.160 Section 114 of the CA 1985 makes contravention of ss 99–104 and 106 a regulatory offence, with liability to a fine for the company and every officer of it who is in default.

2.161 Section 115 of the CA 1985 is a supplementary provision about undertakings to do work or perform services. It has been seen already that there are severe restrictions on the circumstances in which a company may lawfully accept such undertakings in return for the allotment of shares. Section 115 make clear that such an undertaking is enforceable by the company even though the acceptance of it involved a breach of CA 1985, ss 99, 102, 103 or 104, provided of course that it would have been enforceable in the absence of the breach.

2.162 Finally in this area, CA 1985, s 116 provides that ss 99, 101 to 103, 106, 108, 110, 111 and 112–115 apply to a company which has passed and not revoked a resolution to be re-registered under section 43 as a public and to a joint stock company which has passed and not revoked a resolution that the company be a public company in the same way as they apply to a public company. In other words, especially in the case of a private company which has passed a resolution for re-registration but has not yet been re-registered, these provisions apply as if the re-registration had already taken place. It should be noted that CA 1985, s 104 does not apply in these circumstances. As might be expected, given that the two-year period laid down by that section runs only from the date of re-registration. For the other provisions the effect is that the company cannot evade their purpose by anything it does between the date of the resolution and the date of the actual re-registration.

Exemption from section 103

2.163 In *Re Ossory Estates plc*[1] the applicant (the vendor) sold property to the company (the purchaser), consideration being given partly by the allotment of 8 million of the purchasing company's shares. As the company was a public company and was alloting its shares in return for a non-cash consideration, s 103 of the CA 1985 required the property to be independently valued and a report to be made to the company and delivered to the allottee. No such report had been prepared. The vendor sought an order under s 113(2) of the CA 1985 exempting it from liability under s 103. The court granted the order. In considering whether to grant an exemption order the court was required by s 113(5)(a) to have regard to the overriding principle that a company which allots shares should receive money or money's worth at least equal in value to the aggregate of the nominal value of the shares and any premium. The vendor had complied with all the undertakings given on the transfer of property and was likely to continue to do so, so that although the court was required by s 113(3)(a) to take such liability into account it was not on the facts a matter of any weight. The purchaser had sold substantial parts of the property purchased at a profit, and the court was satisfied that the overriding principle had been complied with. In addition, a valuation report complying with s 108 was now available. In the circumstances, it was just and equitable that the vendor should be relieved of any liability under s 103, and the order sought would be granted[2].

1 [1988] BCLC 213, 4 BCC 460, ChD.
2 For a case which, on its facts, went the other way, see *Re Bradford Investments plc (No 2)* [1991] BCLC 688, [1991] BCC 379, ChD (Companies Court).

Commissions and discounts

2.164 As a general proposition it is unlawful for a company to issue shares at a price less than their nominal value (this does not preclude the issue of partly-paid or nil-paid shares, provided that in such cases the company retains the right to claim at least the nominal value). The rule was established in *Ooregum Gold Mining Co of India v Roper*[1] and may be viewed as an application of the capital maintenance doctrine – if the shares are shown in the company's books as fully paid at a certain value, then creditors are entitled to assume that the nominal value at least has been subscribed. However, by way of exception to the general principle, under certain circumstances it is lawful for the company to pay a commission to any person in return for subscribing, or agreeing to subscribe for shares in the company, or procuring or agreeing to procure subscriptions for shares in the company[2]. The conditions which have to be satisfied in order to make this lawful are as follows.

1 [1892] AC 125, HL; see also *Re Eddystone Marine Insurance Co* [1893] 3 Ch 9, CA.
2 CA 1985, s 97.

2.165 The payment of the commission must be authorised by the company's articles (article 4 of Table A gives such authority). The rate of commission must not exceed the lesser of 10% of the price at which the shares are issued and any rate set out in the articles (Table A does not specify a rate). In addition, where the shares are offered to the public, the rate of commission must be set out in the prospectus[1]. Where the shares are not offered to the public, the rate of commission must be disclosed to the Registrar in a notice in the prescribed form signed by every director of the company or his agent authorised in writing. The notice must be delivered to the Registrar before the commission is paid[2]. Where a circular or notice (not being a prospectus within the meaning of the Act) is issued inviting subscription for the shares, the commission must be disclosed in that circular or notice[3]. Failure to comply with s 97 is a regulatory offence, leaving the company and every defaulting officer of it liable to a fine.

1 CA 1985, s 97(3).
2 CA 1985, s 97(3)(a).
3 CA 1985, s 97(3)(b).

2.166 Section 98 of the CA 1985 provides that apart from the cases mentioned in s 97 the use of the company's shares or capital money to pay commissions, discounts or allowances to any person in return for subscribing or agreeing to subscribe for shares in the company or procuring or agreeing to procure subscriptions for shares in the company is unlawful[1]. This applies to indirect payment as well as to direct payment[2] and it is not possible to circumvent the rule by describing the payment as being for work done for the company or by adding it to the purchase price of assets bought by the company or in any other way. The test is one of substance not form[3].

1 CA 1985, s 98(1).
2 CA 1985, s 98(1).
3 CA 1985, s 98(2).

2.167 However, s 98(3) of the CA 1985 confusingly provides that ss 97 and 98 do not affect the power of a company to pay such brokerage as has previously been lawful. There is no explanation of the difference between commissions and discounts on the one hand and brokerage on the other. Nor does the Act give any guidance as to what brokerage could prior to the passing of the Act have been lawfully paid. Section 98(4) provides that anyone who receives payment in money or shares from a company has power to apply any part of the money or shares in payment of any commission, provided that the payment of such commission by the company would in the circumstances have been lawful under CA 1985, s 97.

2.168 The major and obvious deficiency of CA 1985, s 98 is that it gives no indication of the consequences of paying commission in circumstances where this is not permitted. Such payments do not amount to a regulatory offence (the offence in s 97(4) is concerned only with failure to disclose the payment of commission). Presumably, the directors who are party to the payment of the commission are in breach of their duty to the company since they have used the company's funds for an improper purpose. It might also be argued that a person who received commission knowing it to be improper held it on a constructive trust for the company, which could thus reclaim it. However, this point must be regarded as entirely speculative.

FAILURE OF PROPOSED ALLOTMENT

2.169 Proposed allotments of shares may fail for various reasons. Where it is intended that the shares, on issue, shall be listed on a stock exchange, there is the possibility that the application for listing will fail. Section 86 of the CA 1985 deals with this situation. It applies when the prospectus states that application for listing has been or will be made. An allotment made on an application in pursuance of the prospectus (or an agreement to take the shares by a person underwriting an offer[1]) is void if the permission has not been applied for before the third working day after the first issue of the prospectus or, if the permission has been refused, before the expiration of three weeks from the closing of the subscription lists[2]. Within those three weeks the relevant stock exchange may extend the period to not more than six weeks. It appears from the wording of the section that the voidness of the allotment is automatic, ie no allottee has any power to choose to keep the shares.

1 CA 1985, s 86(9).
2 CA 1985, s 86(2).

2.170 Where s 86(2) of the CA 1985 renders the allotment void, the company must forthwith repay to the applicants for shares all moneys received in pursuance of the prospectus[1]. If this requirement is not complied with within eight days of the date when it arises, the directors become personally liable (jointly and severally) to repay the money with interest at 5% per annum. A director may be excused from this liability if he proves that the default in the repayment was not due to any misconduct or negligence on his part[2]. Money received from applicants must be kept in a separate designated bank account so long as there is a possibility that it will have to be repaid (which in practice would appear to mean until the shares are admitted to listing). Failure to do so is a regulatory offence, for which the company and every officer of it who is in default is liable to a fine[3]. Any attempt on the part of the company to require applicants to waive compliance with these provisions is void[4].

1 CA 1985, s 86(4).
2 CA 1985, s 86(5).
3 CA 1985, s 86(6).
4 CA 1985, s 86(7).

2.171 A second possible reason for the failure of a proposed allotment is illustrated by *Re Nanwa Gold Mines Ltd Ballantyne v Nanwa Gold Mines Ltd*[1].In that case the company (a private company), being in financial difficulties, sought to reduce its capital and issue more shares. A circular was sent to shareholders, explaining the scheme and inviting applications. The application form made it clear that the scheme was conditional on, inter alia, getting enough applications. It promised that sums subscribed would be kept in a separate account and that there would be a refund of the money if the scheme failed. The scheme did fail, and a receiver was appointed. The question before the court was whether the money in the account belonged to the company or to those who had applied for shares. It was held that the money was repayable to the persons who had subscribed for shares.

1 [1955] 3 All ER 219, [1955] 1 WLR 1080, ChD.

2.172 The decision in *Re Nanwa Gold Mines* is obviously to be welcomed, but it must be noted that the court reached this conclusion by finding that the applicants had a lien or equity on the money, this being derived from the promises made in the circular and the application form. From this it may be deduced that the money would have belonged to the company in the absence of these promises. In other words there is no general principle that subscribers to an allotment are entitled to their money back if the allotment is not as successful as hoped. Such entitlement has to be derived from a term of the allotment process. Although in theory such a term could be implied, it seems unlikely in practice that a court would be very ready to imply terms of this kind.

Damages for failure to allot

2.173 Where a company breaches a contract to allot a specified number of its shares, and an order for the specific performance of the contract was made, it was established in *Sri Lanka Omnibus Ltd v Perera*[1] that the damages to be awarded to the allotee are restricted to the equivalent of the dividends at the rates declared by the company between the date when the shares should have been allotted and the date of actual allotment, with interest on the dividends until payment.

1 [1952] AC 76, [1951] 2 TLR 1184, PC.

SHARE PREMIUM

The share premium account

2.174 The nominal value is exactly that – it is the value which the shares are nominally declared to have. It need have no relationship to the net asset value per share at the time of issue or to the market price of the shares at any time. The share premium is then the amount by which the price which the company receives for the shares exceeds the nominal value of the shares. The share premium rules apply also where shares are issued for a non-cash consideration the value of which exceeds the nominal value of the shares[1].

1 *Henry Head & Co Ltd v Ropner Holdings Ltd* [1952] Ch 124; *Shearer (Inspector of Taxes) v Bercain Ltd* [1980] 3 All ER 295; but see now CA 1985, ss 131–132.

2.175 The possibility of a share premium raises the question whether the premium element of the subscription price is to be treated as part of the company's issued capital – and thus subject to the capital maintenance doctrine – or whether it is to be regarded as free money of the company.

2.176 Section 130(1) of the CA 1985 requires that the amount of the premium be credited to the share premium account. This account is in principle then treated as part of the share capital of the company, for s 130(2) stipulates that the provisions of the Act relating to the reduction of capital apply to the share premium account as if it were part of the paid-up share capital. Section 130 provides one group of exceptions to this. These exceptions are that the share premium account may be used by the company for any of the following purposes:

(a) paying-up unissued shares to be allotted as fully paid bonus shares;

(b) writing off the company's preliminary expenses;

(c) writing off the expenses of or the commission paid or discount allowed on any issue of shares or debentures of the company.

Merger relief

2.177 Sections 131 and 132 of the CA 1985 go on to provide further exceptions in relation to mergers. Section 131 applies where a company ('the issuing company') has secured at least a 90% equity holding in another company under an arrangement providing for the issuing of equity shares in the issuing company in return for either the issue or transfer to the issuing company of shares (whether equity or non-equity) in the other company or for the cancellation of any shares of the other company not already held by the issuing company. Thus, s 131 can apply to a take-over in which part or all of the consideration paid by the acquiring company takes the form of shares in that company. Although the section is headed 'merger relief' this arrangement is not described in ordinary commercial language as a merger.

2.178 If the equity shares in the issuing company allotted in pursuance of this arrangement are issued at a premium, then CA 1985, s 130 does not apply to those shares (s 131(2)). Clearly, s 130 would normally apply, since it applies generally to shares issued at a premium.

2.179 'Equity shares' for the purposes of this section is defined in CA 1985, s 131(7) as meaning shares comprised in the company's equity share capital. This expression in turn is defined by s 744 of the CA 1985 as meaning:

> '. . . in relation to a company, its issued share capital excluding any part of that share capital which, neither as respects dividends nor as respects capital, carries any right to participate beyond a specified amount in a distribution'.

2.180 Section 132 of the CA 1985 provides further relief from s 130 in the context of group reconstructions. It applies where the company is a wholly-owned subsidiary of another company (referred to in s 132 as 'the holding company') and allots shares to the holding company or another wholly-owned subsidiary of the holding company in consideration for the transfer to the issuing company of assets other than cash, being assets of any company ('the transferor company') which is a member of the group of companies comprising the holding company and all its wholly-owned subsidiaries. To put this convoluted definition into something resembling plain English, the section applies to group reconstructions where one company in the group issues its shares to another group company in return for non-cash assets of another group company (not necessarily the one to which the shares are issued).

2.181 Where CA 1985, s 132 applies and the shares in the issuing company are allotted at a premium, the issuing company need not transfer to its share premium account anything more than the 'minimum premium value'[1]. This is defined[2] as the amount by which the base value of the consideration for the shares allotted exceeds the nominal value of those shares. Section 132(4) then goes on to define the base value of the consideration as the amount by which the base value of the assets transferred exceeds the base value of any liabilities of the transferor company assumed by the issuing company as part of the consideration for the assets transferred. Section 132(5) completes the picture by defining the base value of assets and liabilities for the purposes of s 132(4). The vase value of assets transferred is taken to be the lower of the costs of those assets to the transferor company and the amount at which they were stated in the books of the transferor company immediately before the transfer. The base value of liabilities assumed is taken to be the amount at which they were stated in the transferor company's books immediately before the transfer.

1 CA 1985, s 132(2).
2 CA 1985, s 132(3).

2.182 Where CA 1985, s 132 applies, s 131 does not[1].

1 CA 1985, s 132(6).

2.183 Section 133 of the CA 1985 makes further provision supplementing ss 131 and 132. Section 133(1) provides that a premium on shares which under CA 1985, ss 131 or 132 need not be included in a company's share premium account may also be disregarded in determining the amount at which any shares or other consideration provided for the shares issued is to be included in the company's balance sheet.

PROOF OF OWNERSHIP

2.184 Section 186 of the CA 1985 provides that a share certificate, under the common seal of the company, is prima facie evidence that the person mentioned in it has title to the shares specified in it.

2.185 Section 188 of the CA 1985 deals with share warrants. A company may, if its articles so permit, issue a share warrant stating that the bearer of the warrant is entitled to the shares specified in it. However, the shares in question must be fully-paid shares[1]. A share warrant entitled the bearer to the shares in question[2]. Section 188(2) goes on to say that the shares may be transferred by transfer of the warrant. This form of words is perhaps somewhat misleading. The share warrant is not the same as a share certificate. The bearer of the warrant is not as such a shareholder – the shares have not yet been allotted to him and he will not be entered in the shareholders' register in respect of them. What he has, as s 188(2) rightly says, is the *right* to the shares. Doubtless that right can be transferred by transfer of the warrant. The point is of some importance, for as a general rule it may be said that English law does not recognise bearer shares. This proposition follows from s 185 of the CA 1985, discussed above. Share warrants are not effective as a way to circumvent this requirement, for the holder of a warrant is not as such entitled to exercise any of the rights of a member of a company. He can get that right only by exercising the right conferred by the warrant and converting the warrant into shares, at which point the shares become subject to s 185 and a certificate must be issued.

1 CA 1985, s 188(1).
2 CA 1985, s 188(2).

Chapter 3

Rights attaching to shares

3.1 The rights normally attaching to shares may be divided into three categories, namely the right to vote, the right to participate in dividends and the rights to receive a share of the surplus capital on a winding up.

VOTES

Orders under sections 454 to 457

3.2 These supplemental provisions are related to the basic rights attaching to shares and they deal with the consequences of the making of share restriction orders under the CA 1985, ss 210, 216 or 445.

3.3 Section 454 of the CA 1985 sets out the basic rule. As long as shares are subject to the restrictions of Pt XV of the CA 1985[1], they may not be issued or transferred, nor may votes be cast in respect of them. No further shares in the company may be issued in right of them or in pursuance of any offer made to their holder (this would appear to prohibit pro rata allotments on issue of new shares, as well as bonus, dividend or scrip issues). Moreover, except in a liquidation, no payment may be made of any sums due from the company in respect of them (this covers both dividend payments and any lawful capital payments).

1 For example, CA 1985, ss 454–457.

3.4 Where the above restrictions are in force, any agreement to transfer the shares is void unless it is made in accordance with directions given by the Secretary of State or by the court[1]. The same applies to agreements to transfer the right to be issued with shares in respect of the restricted shares or to receive any payment on them (otherwise than in a liquidation)[2]. Attempted evasions of CA 1985, s 454 restrictions are made a criminal offence by s 455. These evasions may take the form of exercising, or purporting to exercise, any right to dispose of the shares; voting in respect of such shares, or appointing a proxy to do so; failing to notify the fact of the restrictions to some other person whom he knows to be entitled to vote in respect of the shares (either in the case of joint holders or in the case of nominees); entering into an agreement which is void under s 454(2) or (3)[3]. A company which issues shares in contravention of a restriction order (ie which issues shares to a person whose shares are restricted and who is therefore not entitled to receive further shares in right of the existing shares) is liable to a fine, as is every officer of the company who is in default in this respect[4].

1 CA 1985, s 454(2).
2 CA 1985, s 454(3).
3 CA 1985, s 455(1).
4 CA 1985, s 455(2).

3.5 Section 456 of the CA 1985 allows for the relaxation and removal of restrictions imposed under Part XV.

3.6 Section 456(1) of the CA 1985 grants a general liberty to apply to court for an order that shares subject to a restriction order shall no longer be so subject. Although s 456(1) does not say anything about the terms on which such an order may be made, it may be inferred from the subsection that it is intended to confer a general discretion on the court. This view is to some extent supported by the wording of the next subsection.

3.7 Section 456(1A) of the CA 1985 deals with the situation where the court is satisfied that a restriction order unfairly affects the rights of third parties in relation to the shares. In such a case the court may direct that specified acts by named persons shall not be a breach of the restrictions in Part XV of the CA 1985. This power is stated to be in addition to any other order which the court may make under s 456(1), thus supporting the notion that there is a general power to make dispensing orders under s 456(1).

3.8 The very wide, but somewhat vague, wording in CA 1985, s 456(1A) is presumably intended to cover the situation where, for example, an agreement for the sale of the shares has been entered into before the making of the restriction order. If the intending purchaser of the shares has a contract to resell those shares, then he is likely to be prejudiced if the contract is not carried through (though in the case of a listed company there would presumably be good prospects of buying substitute shares in the market place). This might be an example of a case where the intending buyer – an innocent third party in the events which led to the making of a restriction order – would be unduly prejudiced by the strict application of s 454. Of course it is to be assumed that the shares would remain subject to the restriction order in the hands of the new owner, since the scheme of Pt XV is to attach the restrictions to the shares rather than to the owner. However, this is something which the buyer could take into account when deciding to go through with the transaction. In many cases the restriction order will have been imposed because of the conduct of the former owner.

3.9 Locus standi to make an application under s 456 of the CA 1985 varies according to the circumstances. If the restriction order was originally made by the Secretary of State, or if he has refused to make an order disapplying the restrictions, then the application may be made by any person aggrieved (but not by the company itself). If the order was made by the court under s 216 of the CA 1985 (which relates to failure to disclose details of share holdings) the application may be made by any person aggrieved or by the company.

3.10 Section 456(3) of the CA 1985 provides that, except in the case of an order under s 456(1A) – scc above – an order disapplying restrictions may be made by the Secretary of State or by the court if, but only if, the court or the Secretary of State is satisfied that the relevant facts about the shares have been disclosed to the company and no unfair advantage has accrued to any person as a result of the earlier failure to make that disclosure or the shares are to be transferred for valuable consideration and the court (in any case) or the Secretary of State (if the order was made under ss 210 or 445) approves the transfer. This subsection does not apply to an order removing restrictions which have been continued in force under s 456(6)[1].

1 CA 1985, s 456(7).

3.11 Section 456(4) of the CA 1985 gives the court a general power to order the sale of shares which are subject to a restriction order. The application may be made by the Secretary of State (unless the restrictions were imposed under CA 1985, s 216) or by the company. This power differs from the power given by s 456(1A) in that it allows the court to order a forced sale, ie it may be exercised even where the shareholder does not wish to sell the shares. In addition, under s 456(4) the court has power to direct that the shares, once sold, shall cease to be subject to the restrictions. Section 456(5) widens this still further by allowing the court, on an application under s 456(4), to make such further order in relation to the shares as it thinks fit. Under s 456(6) an order removing restrictions from shares under s 456(4) or made with a view to permitting a transfer of the shares may continue the restrictions in relation to the issue of new shares in respect of the restricted shares and/or the restrictions in relation to receiving sums of money from the shares.

3.12 Section 457 of the CA 1985 goes on to make further provisions relating to the sale of restricted shares by court order under CA 1985, s 456(4). The proceeds of sale, less the costs of the sale, are to be paid into court for the benefit of the persons beneficially interested in the shares. Any such person may apply to court for the whole or part of those proceeds to be paid to him[1]. On the making of such an application the court shall order the payment out of sums due to the applicant in respect of the sale of his portion of the shares which were sold (of course this may come to 100% in some cases) together with interest thereon. This is a mandatory provision – the person beneficially interested in the shares is automatically entitled to the proceeds of sale once an application is made[2]. At the same time the court has a discretion, but not a duty, to order that the applicant's costs of making the application shall also be paid out of the proceeds of sale. If an order in these terms is made, the applicant is entitled to payment of those costs before any other person interested receives any part of the proceeds. The practical effect of this will be to reduce the net proceeds available to other interested parties.

1 CA 1985, s 457(1).
2 CA 1985, s 457(2).

3.13 The right to receive notice of meetings, to attend them, speak at them and vote at them is normally considered a basic incident of holding shares. However, there is no provision in the Companies Acts which requires that any of these rights be attached to any particular share, and it is not unknown to find preference shares which carry no voting rights (though the general trend away from preference shares inevitably makes this less common than it once was).

DIVIDENDS

3.14 The right to participate in dividends is commonly regarded as basic to the holding of shares, but it too is not prescribed by the Companies Acts. Just as preference shares often carry a preferential right to dividend, so it is not unknown to find shares which have no right to dividend, often in return for enhanced rights to participate in surplus capital on a winding up.

PARTICIPATION IN CAPITAL

3.15 When a company is wound up, any surplus capital which remains after paying off the company's debts, is returned to the shareholders in proportion to their entitlements to it. Although it is usual for ordinary shares to carry a right to participate in surplus capital, this is again a matter left to the internal regulations of the company. Preference shares sometimes lose the right to such participation in exchange for the enhanced right to dividends which they normally have.

CLASSES OF SHARES

3.16 There is no requirement in the Companies Acts to have more than one class of shares. Indeed, Table A is drafted largely on the assumption that there will be only one class of shares. At the same time it is possible to have shares of separate classes.

Defining classes

3.17 The share capital of the company must be stated in the memorandum. Consequently, if the shares are to be divided into different classes, the division will need to be stated in the memorandum. However, there is no requirement that the memorandum must also contain details of the different rights to be attached to each class. The question of where the rights are set out has important implications for the rules on the changing of class rights, as discussed below.

3.18 The inclusion in the memorandum of different classes of shares is likely to produce a need for alterations to the articles of association, and it will be necessary to consider what changes to the articles are required.

3.19 If separate classes are to be used, it is necessary to consider what the differences between them will be. The answer to this question will inevitably depend on the purposes for which class rights are being introduced. Possible differences include:

- voting rights;
- dividend rights. Where there are different classes of shares it is common to find that one class is designated as 'preference shares' although this term does not appear in the Companies Acts and must be considered as having no strict legal meaning. Where preference shares are used it is common to find that the preference shares carry a right to dividend prior to that of the ordinary shares. This dividend is often, though not always, expressed as a fixed percentage on the nominal value of the shares. This arrangement has both advantages and disadvantages for the holder of the preference shares. The advantage is that they have in effect first claim on the profits and are to that extent in a better position than the holders of the ordinary shares. The disadvantage is that their claim is limited to their fixed percentage, so that even if the company is very successful, they cannot hope to receive larger amounts in dividends (a restriction which does not apply to the holders of the ordinary shares). At the same time both preference shares and ordinary shares are immutably subject to the restriction that no dividends can be declared unless there are profits available for the purpose[1];
- participation in capital on winding up;
- veto rights. One possible use of share classes is to allow particular shareholders to exercise veto rights, either generally or in relation to specified matters. This can be done by providing in the articles that particular resolutions cannot be passed unless approved by the holders of the class in question. Although this technique is generally capable of being effective, it is to be noted that it cannot override mandatory provisions of the Companies Acts providing that resolutions of particular types are effective[2].

1 CA 1985, s 263.
2 Such as CA 1985, s 303 allowing the removal of a director by ordinary resolution. Thus, share classes are not an effective way to protect against this.

3.20 Separate classes of shares do not appear to be as popular as they once were, but they may offer useful ways to structure participation in a company by inactive investors.

What is a 'class right'?

3.21 Curiously, the Companies Acts contain no definition of the term 'class right', although a number of provisions, including CA 1985, s 125, are expressed to apply to companies whose share capital is 'divided into different classes'.

3.22 The only reported case in which the question has been considered at any length is *Cumbrian Newspapers Group Ltd v Cumberland and Westmorland Herald Newspaper and Printing Co Ltd*[1]. In that case the plaintiff company held over 10% of the shares in the defendant company. The defendant's articles of association were altered to give the plaintiff, by name, rights of pre-emption over the other issued shares in the company, rights over the unissued shares and, so long as it held at least 10% of the shares in the defendant, the right to appoint a director of the company. No formal division of the shares into classes was ever made, and it appeared that the rights were personal to the plaintiff in the sense that they could not have been transferred to any purchaser of the plaintiff's shares. Later the defendant company proposed to pass a special resolution at a general meeting in order to deprive the plaintiff company of these rights. This procedure would have been proper if the rights were not class rights, but clearly did not conform to the rules for the variation of class rights. It therefore became necessary to decide whether the rights were class rights. Scott J held that rights conferred in articles of association are to be divided into three categories, as follows:

(a) rights annexed to particular shares, such as dividend rights and rights to participate in surplus assets on a winding up, which, even if defeasible on the transfer of the shares by a named individual, were are clearly 'rights attached to a class of shares';

(b) rights conferred on an individual in a capacity other than a member, eg as a solicitor[2]. These rights are clearly not 'class rights';

(c) rights conferred on a beneficiary as a member of the company but which are not attached to any particular class of shares. Where specific rights are conferred on members in their capacity as members, those members have 'rights attached to a class of shares' and become the holders of a 'class of shares' for the purposes of the rules on the variation of class rights.

Obviously, the rights in this case fell into the third category, and it followed that variation of them required compliance with the CA 1985, s 125 procedure.

1 [1987] Ch 1, [1986] 2 All ER 816, Scott J.
2 As in *Eley v Positive Government Security Life Assurance Co Ltd* (1876) 1 Ex D 88, CA.

3.23 Much of Scott J's analysis in this case is uncontroversial. Categories (a) and (b) were well established before the case, and no one could seriously argue with them. The difficulty is over category (c). Two questions arise. The first is whether such rights are properly described as class rights. Assuming that they are, the second question is how to decide, in a given case, whether the rights are conferred on the beneficiary 'as a member', since it is this feature which alone distinguishes category (c) from category (b).

3.24 On the first of these questions Scott J relied heavily on an anomaly which would arise if such rights were not considered to be class rights. If the rights were contained in the memorandum but there was no procedure for varying them, they would apparently be unalterable, since they would not be class rights and would thus not fall within CA 1985, s 125, whereas if they were in the articles they would apparently be more easily alterable than class rights because the ordinary CA 1985, s 9 special resolution procedure would apply to them. The point is well taken, but it may be doubted whether it is quite as strong as Scott J suggests. The fact is that rights in the memorandum have always been less easily alterable than rights in the articles – that is one of the well-known distinctions between the two documents – and it is thus not so surprising that this difference should exist in relation to category (c) rights. On the other side of the argument is the point that CA 1985, s 125 is expressed to apply where the share capital is divided into shares of different classes. The share capital must of course be stated in the memorandum, and in the case of category (c) rights no such division will be stated in the memorandum (such a statement would move the case out of category (c) and into category (a)). In effect the argument must be that the shares are *impliedly* divided into different classes, albeit that this is done by the articles and not by the memorandum.

3.25 The apparently intractable nature of the dilemma in this case arises from the fact that the rules are simply not written with category (c) rights in mind. Scott J was therefore forced to decide as a matter of policy how such rights should be classified.

3.26 In *Cumbrian Newspapers* it was obvious (indeed undisputed) that the rights had been intended to confer on the plaintiffs protection against certain eventualities, and that the value of this protection would be largely negated if the rights could be taken away under CA 1985, s 9. From that point of view it might fairly be said that the decision gave effect to the intentions of the parties and did justice. It is less clear that this would be so in every category (c) case. It is equally unclear whether this argument really justifies what might well be regarded as doing violence to the words of the Companies Acts.

3.27 On the second difficulty, that of identifying when rights are conferred on a person as a member, Scott J has little to say. He held that *on the facts*, this requirement was satisfied. What is thus left uncertain is how there could be a case where rights were conferred upon a member, but not in that capacity. In *Eley v Positive Government Security Life Assurance Co Ltd*[1] the relevant rights were conferred on the plaintiff at a time when he was not a member of the company, so it was clear that they could not be conferred on him as a member of the company.

1 (1876) 1 Ex D 88, CA.

3.28 In *Cumbrian Newspapers* the issue is more difficult. The rights were conferred on the plaintiff company as part of a deal intended to secure the future of local newspaper publishing in Cumbria. The plaintiff did not get the rights because it was a shareholder. Rather, the rights were agreed for independent commercial reasons, after which the parties, who were clearly familiar with cases such as *Eley*, ensured that the plaintiff got some shares so as to be able to enforce the rights. If this set of facts leads to the conclusion that the rights were conferred on the plaintiff as a shareholder, then there can be very few cases where rights conferred on a shareholder will be held not to have been conferred on him in that capacity. Suppose, for example, that Mr Eley had negotiated a deal under which he was to be the company's secretary and as part of that deal had stipulated that he was to be allotted some shares, together with the inclusion in the articles of the clause allowing him to remain solicitor. Would that right then have been held to have been conferred upon him as a member? On the basis of *Cumbrian Newspapers* the answer appears to be that it would; but if that is right, then the effect of *Eley* can readily be circumvented.

Changing class rights

3.29 In considering the legitimacy from the point of view of the preference shareholders of any change to the articles an important preliminary question is whether the proposed change actually alters the rights of the preference shareholders (as distinct from the merely altering the value of those rights). The best known case in this area is *Greenhalgh v Arderne Cinemas Ltd*[1], where it was proposed to subdivide a class of 10s. shares into 2s. shares. One effect of this would be to deprive the plaintiff of control of the company (he held shares of another class, which would be outvoted by the newly subdivided shares), but the Court of Appeal held that this did not amount to a variation of the rights attaching to the plaintiff's shares, namely the right to have one vote for every share held. It was admitted that as a matter of business reality the value of the plaintiff's rights was seriously adversely affected, but affecting the value of the rights is not the same as affecting the rights themselves. A similar line has been followed in subsequent cases.

1 [1946] 1 All ER 512, CA.

3.30 In *White v Bristol Aeroplane Co Ltd*[1] the capital of the company was £3.9m, consisting of £600,000 preference stock and £3.3m ordinary stock, all of which was issued and fully paid. The articles of association of the company provided:

> '. . . all or any of the rights or privilege attached to any class of shares forming part of the capital for the time being of the company may be affected, modified, varied, dealt with, or abrogated in any manner with the sanction of an extraordinary resolution passed at a separate meeting of the members of that class . . .'

They also provided:

> '. . . preference shares or preference stock shall not confer on the holders thereof the right in respect thereof to receive notice of or to attend or vote at a general meeting unless the dividend thereon is in arrear or unless the meeting is convened to consider a resolution for winding up or to reduce capital or to consider a resolution directly affecting their rights or privileges as a separate class . . .'

1 [1953] Ch 65, [1953] 1 All ER 40, CA.

3.31 The company proposed to create (by way of capitalisation of undistributed profits) (a) 660,000 new cumulative preference shares of £1 each ranking *pari passu* with the existing preference stock, and (b) 2.64m ordinary shares of 10s. each ranking *pari passu* with the existing ordinary stock. Under the company's regulations both new issues would be distributed to existing ordinary stockholders. It was accepted that the rights of existing preference stockholders were not modified, varied or abrogated by the proposal, and that no separate significance should be attached to the term 'dealt with'. On this basis it was held that the proposed transaction would, or might, affect the enjoyment of their rights by the preference stockholders, but their rights as such would not be affected, and, therefore, the proposed transaction could be carried out without the summoning of a separate meeting of the preference stockholders, and without the summoning of the preference stockholders to attend and vote at a general meeting of the company[1].

1 See also *Re Mackenzie & Co Ltd* [1916] 2 Ch 450.

3.32 Similarly, in *Re John Smith's Tadcaster Brewery Co Ltd, the Company v Gresham Life Assurance Society Ltd*[1] the articles of the company provided:

> 'Subject to the provisions of [the Companies Act 1929, s 61, later replaced by the Companies Act 1948, s 72] all or any of the rights or privileges attached to any class of shares forming part of the capital for the time being of the company may be affected, modified, dealt with or abrogated in any manner with the sanction of an extraordinary resolution passed at a separate meeting of the members of that class.'

1 [1953] Ch 308, [1953] 1 All ER 518, CA.

3.33 The directors of the company, of which the issued paid-up capital consisted of £1.74m 5% cumulative preference stock and 1.92m ordinary shares of £1 each, proposed to increase the capital of the company by the creation of 280,000 ordinary shares of £1 each, to capitalise an amount standing to the credit of the company's reserve account, and to apply the same in paying up the new ordinary shares which would then be distributed among ordinary shareholders credited as fully paid. The Court of Appeal held that the proposed transactions did not affect the rights of the preference stockholders within the meaning of article 54.

3.34 Where there is an alteration of the rights of the preference shareholders, it becomes necessary to consider the motivation and justification for the proposal. In *Rights and Issues Investment Trust Ltd v Stylo Shoes Ltd*[1] the plaintiff was an ordinary shareholder in the defendant company. The defendant company had a nominal capital of £2m divided into 8m 5s. shares. Its issued capital consisted of 400,000 management shares and 3.6m ordinary shares. Each management share carried eight votes, so that the management shares carried approximately 47% of the total voting power. The defendant company had been negotiating for the acquisition of the capital of another company. It was proposed, for this purpose to issue the unissued ordinary shares of the defendant company to that company or its shareholders and to create 4.8m new 5s. shares. To give effect to this proposal two meetings were convened. One was a separate meeting of the ordinary shareholders of the defendant company to pass a special resolution approving an increase of the voting rights carried by the management share from eight votes per share to 16 votes per share, and the other meeting was of the shareholders of the defendant company. The effect of the increase in the voting rights attached to a management share would be that the management shareholders would, although they took up no new shares, retain approximately the same voting strength as before. At both meetings management shareholders did not vote in respect of any shares held by them. At the separate meeting of the ordinary shareholders 92% of the votes cast were in favour of altering the voting rights attached to the management shares. At the meeting of all shareholders 96.5% of the votes cast were in favour of the increase of capital; 89% of the votes cast were in favour of increasing the voting rights of management shares.

1 [1965] Ch 250, [1964] 3 All ER 628, ChD.

3.35 On the plaintiff's application for an interlocutory injunction to restrain the defendant company from carrying the resolutions into effect, on the ground that their effect would be oppressive on the ordinary shareholders, it was held that there had not been discrimination against, or oppression of, the ordinary shareholders, for a decision by the members of the defendant company, other than holders of management shares. That it would benefit the defendant company if the present basis of control continued, notwithstanding that the management shares would represent a smaller proportion of the issued capital than before, was a proper decision to make on a matter of business policy. There is no principle of law which prevents the members of a company from altering the voting rights attached to shares provided that the alteration is sanctioned by the members in accordance with the constitution of the company, in good faith and for the benefit of the company as a whole. The plaintiff's action therefore failed.

Other actions

3.36 In relation to proposed courses of action other than variations of the articles it may also be necessary to examine carefully both the general law and the provisions of the articles in order to establish exactly what are the rights of various categories of shareholder. This is well illustrated by *Dimbula Valley (Ceylon) Tea Co Ltd v Laurie*[1]. In that case the share capital of a company was divided into ordinary shares and preference shares. The original articles of association provided:

> 'The 10,000 preference shares in the original capital shall confer on the holders the following rights: (a) The right to receive out of the profits of the company a cumulative preferential dividend at the rate of 6% pa on the amount for the time being paid up thereon, such dividend to commence as from March 31 1896. (b) The right in the event of the company being wound up to be paid out of the surplus assets of the company, the amount paid up in respect of such preference shares and all arrears (if any) of dividend thereon up to the date of the commencement of the winding up in priority to the other shareholders, and to participate in any further surplus assets of the company after payment of the amount paid up in respect of the other shares rateably with the other shareholders in proportion to the amount paid-up on the said preference shares and the other shares respectively.'

1 [1961] Ch 353, [1961] 1 All ER 769.

3.37 The original articles also provided:

> 'Subject to the rights of members entitled to shares issued upon special conditions, the

profits of the company, after setting aside such sum to a reserve as the directors may decide, shall be divisible among the members in proportion to the amount paid-up on the shares held by them respectively . . .'

3.38 Another article empowered the directors to place profits to reserves. The original articles contained no capitalisation provision and no article in terms authorising the declaration of dividends, but the declaration of dividends was included among the business to be transacted at ordinary general meetings of the company. Later the company adopted new articles, which included a capitalisation article. Certain questions arose concerning participation by preference shareholders in surplus assets on winding up, and whether under the new capitalisation article the company had power to allot shares credited as fully paid-up to ordinary shareholders by way of capitalisation of reserves resulting from revaluation of capital assets. It was held that in a winding up the preference shareholders would, pursuant to art 5(b), be entitled to participate rateably with the ordinary shareholders in the assets of the company remaining after payment of the debts and liabilities of the company, after payment of any arrears of preference dividend up to the date of the beginning of the winding up, after returning to the members the amounts paid up or credited as paid-up on all the shares of the company and after providing for costs.

3.39 Moreover, a reserve fund resulting from revaluation of unrealised fixed assets, made in good faith by competent valuers and unlikely to be liable to short term fluctuations might legally be capitalised, or might be distributed legally as dividend where the regulations of the company so permitted. Accordingly the new capitalisation article authorised capitalisation of the capital surplus resulting from the revaluation and, as this surplus could legitimately have been distributed as dividend (eg, exclusively among the ordinary shareholders), a capitalisation exclusively for their benefit did not encroach on rights of the preference shareholders and would be valid.

Meaning of 'preference shares' etc

3.40 It is a curious but undeniable fact that the Companies Acts do not mention the term 'preference share' or any synonym for it. The phrase has no precise legal meaning, but it is interesting to consider the case of *Re Powell-Cottons's Resettlement, Henniker-Major v Powell-Cotton*[1]. This was a trusts case, in which the investment clause in a settlement permitted investment in (among other things) 'the debentures debenture stock or rent-charge guaranteed or preferred stock or shares of any company incorporated by special Act or by or under any public general Act or Acts of the Imperial Parliament' and also in 'the ordinary stock or shares of any such company a fixed or minimum rate of interest or dividend on which is guaranteed by the government of the United Kingdom . . . and in or upon ordinary preferred stock or shares but not on deferred stock or shares of any such company . . .' It was accepted that a preferred stock was a stock which had some preference or priority over the ordinary or common stock. On the question of the meaning of 'ordinary preferred stock' in this clause it was held that 'ordinary preferred stock' was a sub-class of ordinary stock which had some preference or priority over another sub-class of ordinary stock, and bore the same meaning as the commercial description 'preferred ordinary stock'[2].

1 [1957] Ch 159, [1957] 1 All ER 404, ChD.
2 *Andrews v Gas Meter Co* [1897] 1 Ch 361, 66 LJ Ch 246.

Meaning of 'variation' in relation to preference shares

3.41 In *House Of Fraser plc v ACGE Investments Ltd*[1] a special resolution was passed reducing the company's capital by paying off and cancelling the cumulative preference shares. No class meetings of preference shareholders were held to approve or disapprove the reduction. The company presented a petition to the Second Division of the Inner House of the Court of Session under s 136(1) of the CA 1985 asking that the reduction of capital be confirmed. Answers to the petition were lodged by the registered owners of a number of the preference shares, who contended, inter alia, that the failure to hold class meetings of the preference shareholders was in contravention of their rights under the articles of association of the company, art 12 of which provided for such a meeting if the shares were 'modified, commuted, affected or dealt with'. The Second Division confirmed the reduction of capital, and this decision was affirmed by the House of Lords, which said that the proposed cancellation of preference shares involved the fulfilment and satisfaction of the contractual rights of the shareholders including the return of capital in priority to other shares; and that, since there had been no variation of those rights, no agreement between the company and the holders in terms of art 12 of the company's articles of association was necessary to effect the reduction of capital[2].

1 [1987] AC 387, [1987] 2 WLR 1083, HL.
2 See also *Re Saltdean Estate Co Ltd* [1968] 1 WLR 1844.

3.42 By contrast, in *Re Northern Engineering Industries plc*[1] the company's articles of association provided that the rights attached to any class of shares should be deemed to be varied by 'the reduction of the capital paid up on such shares'. The company proposed to reduce its capital by paying off the preference shares and cancelling them. The company argued that it did not have to obtain the class consent to the reduction since the provision making a reduction a variation of class rights did not apply since it only applied to a reduction to a figure which was in excess of zero. It was held that the effect of the articles was to make the proposed reduction and cancellation a variation of the class rights of the shareholders for which the consent of the classes of preference shareholders was required. Since this consent had not been given, the reduction would not be confirmed by the court as it had not been carried out in accordance with the company's articles of association.

1 [1993] BCLC 1151, [1993] BCC 267, ChD.

Procedure

3.43 The rules on the procedure for changing class rights are extremely and unnecessarily complex. The exact details of the procedure to be followed depend upon the combination of where the class rights are written down and where (if anywhere) provisions for the variation of those rights appear. The various combinations are as follows.

Rights not in memorandum; no variation provision in articles

3.44 Section 125(2) of the CA 1985 applies to this case. A change in the class rights requires the consent (in writing or at an Extraordinary General Meeting of the class) of the holders of three-quarters in nominal value of the issued shares of that class. In addition it is necessary to comply with any further requirement as to the variation of the class rights. Given that such a further provision can by definition not appear in the articles, it seems most likely that it will appear in the memo. On a literal reading of the words of the subsection it would appear that a requirement contained, for example, in a shareholders' agreement would be caught by this subsection, but this is open to obvious objection, since it allows a small minority of shareholders to impose further restrictions on the variation of the rights. One way out of this dilemma would be to say that the further restriction must be one which is binding on the company. This would exclude the case of a shareholders' agreement, since the company is not normally a party to such agreements. On the other hand, it does leave a question as to what other restriction there might be, which would be validly binding on the company. This problem is exacerbated by the fact that it is normally understood that the company cannot by any external agreement restrict its power to alter its articles, even where the making of such an alteration would be a breach of contract on the part of the company[1]

Rights in memorandum or elsewhere

3.45 Variation provisions in memorandum or elsewhere and variation is connected with giving, variation, revocation or renewal of CA 1985, s 80 authority or reduction of share capital under Ca 1985, s 135. In this case s 135(3) applies. The variation requires:

(a) the agreement of holders of 75% of the class of shares whose rights are being varied. The agreement may be given at a meeting of the holders of the shares of that class or may be given in the form of a written resolution signed by the consenting shareholders; and

(b) compliance with any further requirement for variation contained in the memorandum or articles. An oddity of the wording of this subsection is that where the variation provisions are contained otherwise than in the memorandum or articles (assuming that there is anywhere else that they could validly appear) it is apparently unnecessary to comply with those provisions to the extent that they go beyond the requirement of the 75% majority contained in s 135(3).

Rights in memorandum; variation provisions in original articles

3.46 In this case the reference to 'original articles' means the articles which were adopted when the company was first incorporated. In this case the only permitted method of variation is that laid down in the articles[1].

1 CA 1985, s 125(4).

Rights elsewhere than in memorandum; variation provision in articles (whenever inserted)

3.47 This case is also covered by s 125(4) of the CA 1985. Again the only permitted method of variation is that laid down in the articles.

Rights in memorandum; no variation procedure in memorandum or articles

3.48 This case is dealt with in the CA 1985, s 125(5). In these circumstances, variation of the class rights requires the consent of all members. It follows that this combination offers by far the best chance of protecting the holders of class rights against unwelcome variations – any holder of the class right will necessarily be a member of the company and thus will have a veto right on any proposed change.

3.49 Apart from any procedure for change laid down in the articles it is necessary to have a class meeting, at which any proposed change to the rights is approved by special resolution. Even then holders of 15% of the class (not being people who consented to or voted for the change) can petition the court to annul the change. The petition objecting to the change must be presented within 21 days of the change being made.

3.50 The CA 1985 gives only somewhat Delphic guidance on the approach to be adopted in the case of an objection. Section 127(4) of the CA 1985 says that the court may disallow the variation if satisfied that it would unfairly prejudice the shareholders of the class represented by applicant. Otherwise the court must confirm the variation. One peculiarity here is that even where the classes represented by the applicant is unfairly prejudiced, it appears that the court retains a discretion as to whether or not to disallow the variation. It is hard to see how it could ever be appropriate to confirm a variation which had been shown to be unfairly prejudicial.

3.51 Another totally unresolved question is how CA 1985, s 127(4) relates to s 459 with its broader test of unfairly prejudicial conduct. Section 126 of the CA 1985 says only that s 125(2), (5) do not derogate from the court's powers under ss 459–461, but this does not deal with all the issues which may arise. Presumably the position is that a s 459 application can be made even though the procedural requirements of s 125 have been satisfied. This seems logical, since there could be cases where the substantive fact of the alteration amounted to unfairly prejudicial conduct, the alteration being made for an improper purpose. This conclusion is reinforced by the fact that s 461(3) expressly alludes to the possibility that a s 461 order might forbid the making of any, or a specified, alteration to the articles. What is much less clear is the relationship between CA 1985, ss 127 and 459. Given that s 127 provides a clear statutory procedure for objecting to an alteration, why is it appropriate to use s 459 instead? It might be supposed that the presence of s 127 would preclude a s 459 application in such cases, but, as already explained, that is inconsistent with CA 1985, s 461(3). It appears that an aggrieved class shareholder has the choice whether to petition under CA 1985, s 127 or under s 459. Which is the more appropriate tactical choice would appear to depend primarily on which remedy is desired. If the petitioner wants the cancellation of the alteration, then s 127 is adequate.

3.52 It might be thought that CA 1985, s 459 should be used in every case, since cancellation of the alteration is also available under that section. In fact, there is a serious danger in using s 459 where the petitioner wants only cancellation. Given the very wide discretion of the court under s 461, there is always the danger that an alternative remedy may be ordered. Since by far the most common remedy is s 459 petitions is an order for the buy-out of the petitioner's shares[1], the petitioner needs to think carefully before using s 459 when s 127 is also available.

1 See Law Com No 246 *Shareholders Remedies*.

3.53 Of course, if a buy-out is the desired solution, then, subject to any put option in the articles or in a shareholders' agreement, CA 1985, s 459 will be the only appropriate mechanism. It is interesting to note that there are apparently no modern reported cases on CA 1985, s 127. The provision is apparently largely a dead letter, partly because the need for 75% approval in the first place reduces the number of cases where there will be 15% who feel strongly enough to litigate, partly because objections are now more likely to come under s 459.

Chapter 4

Transferring shares

SHARE TRANSFERS

Procedures

4.1 The Stock Transfer Act 1963 allows shares in any limited company to be transferred by the completion of a Stock Transfer Form[1], upon which the requisite stamp duty should be paid. The form is then submitted to the company secretary for registration of the transfer. That registration takes the form of entering the new shareholders in the company's Register of Members (and making the necessary adjustments to the entry of the vendors of the shares). A new share certificate should also be issued, although there is no legal requirement to have share certificates at all.

1 In the form set out in Sch 1 to the Act. The Stock Transfer Act 1982 dispenses with the need for a written instrument at all where the transfer is performed electronically through a recognised stock Exchange.

Restrictions

4.2 It is common in private companies to find that the articles of association contain restrictions on the transferability of the shares[1]. Many such companies are in reality quasi-partnerships, in which the members have entered into the corporate relationship on the basis of mutual trust and confidence. Just as it would be inappropriate to allow a partner to sell his share to an outsider without the consent of the other partners, so it is inappropriate to allow a shareholder in a quasi-partnership company to do the same thing. However, Table A contains no restriction on the transferability of shares. It is for each company to decide what solution it prefers, and to adopt special articles which achieve that effect. A word of warning is appropriate at this point. The courts have tended to take a somewhat critical attitude to attempts to restrict the transferability of shares, and the law reports contain more than a few examples of failed attempts at restrictive drafting[2].

1 Before 1948 it was a legal requirement that the articles of a private company contain such a restriction.

2 These include *Victorine Roberts v Letter 'T' Estates Ltd* [1961] AC 795, [1961] 3 WLR 176, PC.

General principles on restricting transferability of shares

4.3 An instructive case on the general approach to be taken to articles purporting to restrict the right to transfer shares is *Stothers v William Steward (Holdings) Ltd*[1], where it was said that in approaching the task of construing the articles, the court was guided by the following general considerations:

(a) shares, being personal property were prima facie transferable and if the right to transfer was to be taken away it was to be done by language of sufficient clarity in the articles;

(b) the articles, including the regulations of Table A incorporated in the articles, had to be construed together and effect given, so far as possible, to every provision; it was only if the express articles were inconsistent with the incorporated regulations of Table A that the former would override the latter;

(c) there was a distinction, well-recognised in company law, between the transfer of shares and their transmission on death.

1 [1994] 2 BCLC 266, sub nom *Re William Steward (Holdings) Ltd* [1994] BCC 284, CA, Civil Division.

4.4 It appears also that references to transfers of shares will normally be understood as referring only to transfer of the legal title, rather than to transfers affecting only the beneficial interest. This may be deduced from *Safeguard Industrial Investments Ltd v National Westminster Bank Ltd*[1], where the bank, acting as executor, was registered as holder of shares. On the completion of the administration of the estate it regarded itself as holding the shares for the beneficiaries absolutely, but did not propose to seek a transfer of the registered ownership. It was held that this did not bring the special articles on transfer of shares into operation.

1 [1982] 1 All ER 449, [1982] 1 WLR 589, CA.

Absolute discretion

4.5 The most draconian approach is to allow the directors absolute discretion to refuse to register transfers of shares to a person of whom they do not approve. In theory such a provision could allow the directors to refuse to register a transfer to a person who already holds shares in the company. They may wish that he was not a shareholder at all, or they may take the view that it is undesirable that his shareholding should be increased.

4.6 Where the power of the directors to refuse to register share transfers is required to be exercised within a certain time (as is the case under art 25 of

Table A) failure to exercise that power within the specified time will result in the power being lost, so that the directors have no option but to register the transfer. This was established in *Re Swaledale Cleaners Ltd*[1].

1 [1968] 3 All ER 619, [1968] 1 WLR 1710, CA.

4.7 Companies should be wary of using a special article which declares that in the case of a proposed transfer the directors 'will' take the shares at a fair value. As was shown in *Rayfield v Hands*[1], the effect of this can be to create a binding contractual obligation on the directors to take the shares, at least where the holding of shares is a requirement for directors[2]. The fact that this conclusion is operative only where there is a requirement to hold shares means that it will rarely be relevant in a public company (where share transfer restrictions are in any case much less common). Indeed, as the judge in *Rayfield v Hands* observed, the principle may well in practice be limited to quasi-partnership companies.

1 [1960] Ch 1, [1958] 2 All ER 194.
2 This point is important because the articles form a contract between the *members*, so a director who was not a member could not be a party to the contract.

4.8 A further restriction on the exercise of this discretion by the directors is the usual overriding requirement that the powers of the directors must be exercised bona fide in the best interests of the company. The attitude of the courts on this point was explored in *Popely v Planarrive Ltd*[1]. P submitted shares for registration in his name, which, if registered, would have given him control of the company as a shareholder. It was clear that if P obtained such control he would thereupon use his power to obtain control of the board. The articles of association provided that the directors of the company had an absolute discretion to refuse to register a transfer of shares. The articles also provided that, if the directors refused to register a transfer of shares, they should send to the transferee, within two months after the date on which the transfer was lodged, notice of their refusal to register the transfer. The directors refused to register the ten shares in P's name but did not inform P of their decision. P sought to have the share register rectified pursuant to s 359 of the CA 1985. The court assumed that the directors' refusal to register the shares in P's name was taken within two months of his request having been submitted to the company, with the result that there were no grounds for applying the principle in *Re Swaledale Cleaners Ltd*. Different considerations apply where the decision is taken within a reasonable time but there is a failure to inform the transferee of the decision. Such a failure may well expose the directors to civil or criminal liability but cannot not relate back to turn the proper exercise of the directors' powers into a nullity. Accordingly, the failure to comply with art 25 could not result in the directors' refusal to register being ineffective.

1 [1997] 1 BCLC 8 (Companies Court), ChD.

4.9 A transferee who alleges that the directors have not acted bona fide in the interests of the company bears the onus of proving this. In private companies, directors will normally have their own personal views as to the suitability of new shareholders, and the court will give them considerable latitude in forming and applying their views.

4.10 If this approach is considered too restrictive, an alternative is to allow shareholders to transfer shares freely to members of their immediate family (a phrase which needs to be defined carefully if this approach is to be adopted) whilst requiring directors' consent for other transfers. This system is most commonly used where a company has been set up by two or more families. Although there may be several individual shareholders, it is likely that the participants conceive of the company of being divided among a number of families in specified proportions. On this basis there is no reason why a readjustment of the shareholdings within one of the families concerned should be of interest to the directors, but a change which brings in a shareholder from outside the existing families, or which shifts the balance of power between the families is a matter of some concern to the directors.

4.11 Where the company is not divided between families in this way another possible approach is to include a pre-emption clause in favour of other existing shareholders or of the directors themselves. Under this system a shareholder wishing to sell his shares must first offer them to other shareholders or to the directors. If a clause of this kind is used, it is necessary to include clear and appropriate provisions about valuation of the shares. Merely requiring the sale to be at a 'fair value' is too vague to work satisfactorily, whilst a provision allowing the directors to fix the value is almost certain to lead to difficulties, since the directors are unlikely to be indifferent as to who gets the shares, and are always vulnerable to allegations of bad faith in the valuation. The only satisfactory approach here is to provide for some independent valuation.

4.12 Some differences of detail arise according to who has the pre-emption rights under the articles, or shareholder agreement, and who is the intending purchaser of the shares. Where the pre-emption rights are in favour of other shareholders, it is usual to provide that they apply only where it is proposed to sell to someone who is not already a shareholder. Where the rights are in favour of the directors, they often apply even to sales to existing shareholders. One possible defect with a transfer article giving pre-emption rights to directors is that the rights can only be invoked if the directors have the cash to pay for the shares at the time when the offer is made. If they do not, then the transferor is effectively freed from any restriction on the transfer.

4.13 An illustration of the problems which can arise from articles of this kind is to be found in *Tett v Phoenix Property and Investment Co Ltd*[1]. The articles of association of the company permitted a member without prior authorisation to transfer his shares to members of his family, and a similar right was given with respect to the transmission of a deceased member's shares to his personal representatives, trustees under his will or his family. They provided that in the case of a proposed transfer outside these categories the transferring shareholder could not transfer his shares to an outsider if any member or the wife, husband, parent or adult child of any member was willing to purchase the shares; they also made provision for settling the fair value at which such shares should be transferred. The directors were authorised, in their absolute discretion and without assigning any reason therefore, to decline to register any transfer outside the permitted categories if the pre-emption rights had not been respected.

1 [1986] BCLC 149, 2 BCC 99, 140, CA.

4.14 The executors of a deceased shareholder sought to sell her interest in the company. She had been the registered holder of 90 shares in the company and was entitled to 23 shares as the beneficiary of a trust which held shares in the company. The executors informed the company's secretarial department that they wished to have the shares sold. They intended that this instruction should relate to the 90 shares but the secretarial department considered that it related only to the 23 shares to be distributed under the trust. A circular was sent to the shareholders but this, because of the confusion, informed the shareholders that only the 23 shares were being offered for sale. The executors took the view that their offer to sell the 90 shares had been rejected in that the only offer they received was one to purchase the shares (ie the 23 shares, not the 90) at an inadequate value. Subsequently the executors agreed to sell all the shares to the plaintiff, who was not a member of the company, the parties assuming that there had been compliance with the pre-emption provisions in the company's articles of association. The secretarial department was informed of this agreement. The transfer of the shares to the plaintiff was later executed and submitted for registration, but the company refused to register it on the grounds that the shares had not been offered to the company's shareholders as was required by its articles of association. At a board meeting it was decided to notify the shareholders that 90 shares were being offered for sale but the board did not consider the plaintiff's application to have the transfer of those shares registered. A circular offering the shares was sent to the shareholders, and one member at least indicated willingness to purchase the shares.

4.15 The question was whether the earlier purported transfer to the plaintiff was entitled to registration. It was held that the articles were effective to cut down the right of a shareholder to transfer his shares. The restriction was not void as being unworkable, since a term could be implied into the article to give it business efficacy requiring a shareholder wishing to transfer his shares to an outsider to take reasonable steps to give notice of that intention to those to whom notice had to be given and to allow a reasonable opportunity for such persons to express their willingness to buy the shares. The requirement of reasonable notice would be satisfied as far as non-members (ie relatives of members who were not themselves members) were concerned if notice was given to members and they were left to pass it on to non-members.

4.16 On the facts, the executors had not given reasonable notice of their intention to transfer the deceased shareholder's 90 shares as none of the correspondence which they had with the company constituted notice of an intention to transfer the shares. Accordingly, the directors were not entitled to register the transfer, since the specified procedures for making an offer to family members had not been complied with, although the decision is obviously correct on the facts of the case.

4.17 Another solution which has proved both popular and problematic is that in which the company's articles provide that a shareholder wishing to transfer shares is bound to offer them to the directors at a fair price to be fixed by the auditors and that the directors are constituted the vendor's agents to effect the sale of the shares. It is the agency provision in this approach which gives rise to particular difficulties.

4.18 In *Munro v Bogie*[1] the plaintiffs had sold their shares under such an arrangement, the shares ultimately being bought by the managing director of the company. The plaintiffs alleged that the auditors had not been instructed to establish the fair value and the purchasers had paid a price based on the total value of the company's assets in its accounts. The directors had known that that value was materially understated and had concealed that fact from them. The director, as their agent, had been under a duty to disclose that fact to them. The director and the companies denied that the auditor had not stated a fair price and also disputed that the director had owed any duty of disclosure. The articles had created only a limited agency in which the price was to be fixed by a third party. The director and the company sought to have the action struck out as disclosing no ground of action. It was held that the articles *might*, in creating the agency, have imposed a duty of disclosure on the directors.

1 [1994] 1 BCLC 415, Ct of Sess (Outer House).

4.19 As *Munro* is reported only on the application to strike out the claim, it cannot be used as authority for the proposition that there is always a duty of disclosure on the directors in such circumstances. Nevertheless, the facts of the case do highlight the problems arising from the use of the concept of agency in the article in question. The advantage of using agency is obvious – it gives the directors authority to bind the vendors in entering into a sale of the shares. The disadvantage is that it threatens to bring with it the fiduciary duties attaching to agents. Obviously this will not matter where the directors act in good faith and do not purchase the shares for themselves, but it will inevitably impose on the directors more extensive duties than they would otherwise have had.

4.20 Where the company has a transfer article of the first kind mentioned above, it is open to the directors to veto any transfer of shares if they do not approve of it, provided of course that they can justify their refusal as being in the best interests of the company.

4.21 Where the articles have more liberal arrangements regarding a transfer to an existing member than regarding a transfer to a non-member, one possible solution is to arrange for the shares to be transferred to an existing member, subject to equitable obligations in favour of a third party. This approach was adopted in *Theakston v London Trust plc*[1]. The articles of the company required the directors to register any transfer to six defined classes of persons one of which was a transfer 'to any other member of the company'. Article 7 laid down provisions for pre-emption where a transfer was not within the six defined classes. It obliged, inter alia, any person 'proposing to transfer any shares' to give a 'transfer notice' to the company and if the company found a purchaser from amongst its members, the transferor had the option of selling the shares or withdrawing the transfer notice. If no purchaser was found, there was a right to sell to any person. One shareholder sought and found a third party purchaser for its shares. In order to circumvent the requirements of the articles an agreement was reached whereby the shares were to be transferred to another shareholder, the purchase being financed by the third party. The transferee agreed with the third party that he would:

(a) endeavour to have the shares registered in his name;

(b) charge the shares in favour of the third party;

(c) vote the shares as directed by the third party;

(d) account to the third party with respect to any distributions received in connection with the shares; and

(e) accept any offer for the shares as and when made by the third party and endeavour to have the third party registered as the owner of the shares.

As regards this last aspect of the agreement, it was provided that where the shareholder served a notice of transfer with respect to the shares and an offer to buy his shares was made, the shareholder was obliged to withdraw his transfer notice and submit a fresh notice of transfer.

1 [1984] BCLC 390, BCC 99,095, ChD.

4.22 The loan from the third party was interest free and was not repayable until the third party had acquired the shares or they had been sold by the shareholder in accordance with the third party's instructions. The shareholder sought to have the share register of the company rectified under s 116 of the Companies Act 1948 so as to delete the name of the vendor from the register and have his name entered instead with respect to its holdings. Another shareholder, who objected to the involvement of the third party in the company, commenced an action seeking, inter alia, a declaration that the agreement between the shareholder and the third party was in breach of the company's articles of association and also seeking damages for conspiracy and inducement of breach of contract. The motion and the action were heard together.

4.23 The court ordered the register of the transfer of the shares. It was said that the reference to 'transfer' in art 6, the article which obliged the directors to register certain types of transfer, referred to an instrument of transfer passing the legal interest in shares and the word 'member' in art 6(vi) referred to a person who had agreed to take shares and who was already a registered member of the company. The agreement for the transfer of the shares registered in the name of the vendor was one between the vendor and the shareholder and was not an agreement between the vendor and the third party, with the shareholder merely acting as a trustee to hold the shares for the third party. Accordingly, as a valid instrument of transfer had been presented with respect to a transfer of shares to a member, the directors of the company were obliged to register the transfer, and the fact that the shares were subject to an equitable obligation did not constitute a sufficient justification for refusing to register the transfer. In addition the shareholder was not a person proposing to transfer his shares within the terms of art 7 of the company's articles of association. There was no unequivocal obligation on the part of the shareholder to execute an instrument of transfer as, among other things, there was the possibility that when the shareholder served on the company a notice of transfer he would subsequently withdraw it if the company found a purchaser for his shares, as was provided for in his agreement with the third party[1].

1 See also *Addiscombe Garden Estates Ltd v Crabbe* [1958] 1 QB 513, [1957] 3 All ER 563, CA; *Greenhalgh v Mallard* [1943] 2 All ER 234, CA; *KCA v Trewhella* (17 December 1979, unreported) Fox J; *Lyle & Scott Ltd v Scot's Trustees* 1958 SC 230, Ct of Sess; revsd [1959] AC 763, [1959] 2 All ER 661, HL; *Owens v GRA Property Trust Ltd* (10 July 1978, unreported) Browne-Wilkinson J; *Prenn v Simmonds* [1971] 3 All ER 237, [1971] 1 WLR 1381, HL; *Safeguard Industrial Investments Ltd v National Westminster Bank Ltd* [1982] 1 All ER 449, [1982] 1 WLR 589, CA; *Samuel v Jarrah Timber and Wood Paving Corpn Ltd* [1904] AC 323, 73 LJ Ch 526, HL.

4.24 The logic of this decision appears to be that references to transfers are to be construed in a purely formalistic way, with the result that an outsider can in effect obtain a foothold in the company by securing the compliance of an existing shareholder, since the court will apparently not take notice of a purely equitable obligation undertaken by the transferee in favour of a third party. The position might possibly be different if the transferee had undertaken to transfer the shares on to the third party, though of course in that event the company would still have the option of refusing to register the subsequent transfer.

4.25 In general the courts will insist that the company substantially complies with any procedure laid down in the articles with respect to share transfers. This can have unfortunate effects on proposed transferees, as is illustrated by the New Zealand case of *Curtis v JJ Curtis & Co Ltd*[1]. The articles of association of the defendant company provided that a shareholder who wished to transfer shares to an outsider was required to give the directors a transfer notice in which he notified them of his intention to sell and specified the sum he fixed as a fair value of the share or shares.

1 [1986] BCLC 86, NZCA.

4.26 By this notice the company was constituted the retiring shareholder's agent for the sale of the shares. The shares comprised in the transfer notice were to be offered first to the members other than the retiring shareholder in proportion to the shares held by them. If, within one calendar month after service of the transfer notice, the directors found a member or any person to purchase the shares the retiring shareholder would be bound to transfer the shares on payment of the fair value. If the directors could not find a member or person to purchase the shares within one calendar month after being served with the transfer notice, the retiring shareholder was at liberty to sell and transfer the shares, or those not placed, to any person at any price[1]. After transfer notices were served the directors misapplied the procedure in the articles by issuing a circular inviting bids for the shares from existing shareholders but without offering them in proprition to the existing shareholdings. The plaintiff was a shareholder who sought to restrain the company from registering transfers arising out of the botched application of the transfer procedure.

1 This appears to have the odd effect of allowing a shareholder to serve a transfer notice specifying an obviously excessive price for the shares, then sell them to someone else for a lesser price when no existing shareholder is prepared to pay the excessive price. It may be doubted whether this was quite the intention.

4.27 The Court of Appeal in New Zealand held that the clear object of the articles was to restrict the rights of members to sell except to other members or within their own families. There must be at least substantial compliance with the procedure laid down in the article as to offers to members before the retiring shareholder was at liberty to sell under art 3(e). Without this a shareholder denied pre-emptive rights had standing to claim an appropriate injunction. Here there had not been substantial compliance. Not only were some of the shares never offered to the plaintiff at all, but, as regards those shares that were offered, an offer to all members of all or any, was materially different from an offer of a definite proportion of each parcel; and it could well evoke a different response. The shareholders desirous of transferring to an outsider had not acquired that right and, although that was through no fault of their own, they could have no equity to set against the plaintiff's claim to an injunction[1]. Although this is a decision of a New Zealand court, the logic appears equally applicable in English law.

1 See also *Black White & Grey Cabs Ltd v Fox* [1969] NZLR 824, NZCA; *Craine v Colonial Mutual Fire Insurance Co Ltd* (1920) 28 CLR 305; *Edmonds v TJ Edmonds Ltd* [1937] NZLR 135 NZSC; on appeal [1937] NZLR 527, NZCA; *Greenhalgh v Mallard* [1943] 2 All ER 234, CA; *Neylon v Dickens* [1978] 2 NZLR 35, PC.

Effect of improper transfer

4.28 If a transfer is made in defiance of restrictions in the articles, the directors are entitled to refuse to register it, in which case the original holder remains the legal owner. He alone is entitled to receive dividends and notices of meetings, and to attend and speak at such meetings. Presumably he holds all these rights on trust for the transferee who is the beneficial owner of the shares.

4.29 Where directors do exercise a power to veto a share transfer (whatever the details of the provision giving them that power) the effect is that the transfer will not be recorded in the company's register of shareholders and the intended transferee will not therefore become the legal owner of the shares. However, if a Stock Transfer Form is executed, this will be an effective assignment of the equitable interest in the shares. The resulting separation of the legal and equitable interests in the shares will create a trust, in which the transferor becomes the trustee, whilst the transferee becomes the beneficiary. The shares are thus held for the benefit of the beneficiary on a bare trust. The transferor must exercise his membership rights in the company for the benefit of the transferee and in accordance with any instructions given by the transferee. The transferee is also entitled to any dividends which may be declared on the shares.

4.30 However, the company is not obliged to deal with the transferee; indeed, it cannot properly do so, since the transferee does not become a member of the company. The transferor is still a member of the company, and is therefore the person entitled to receive information about the company and to attend its meetings (though he could appoint the transferee as his proxy). The company will pay the dividends to the transferor, though he will of course be obliged to hand them over to the transferee. This is obviously an untidy and unsatisfactory state of affairs, and it is no doubt for this reason that few purchasers will accept a transfer of the shares unless they are first assured that they will be recognised and registered by the directors.

Effect of forged transfers

4.31 A forged document is normally a nullity[1], and the true owner of the shares is entitled to have the share register rectified if the purported allottee has been entered on it. It appears that a forged transfer cannot appear anywhere in a valid chain of title. Although the effects of this may seem draconian from the point of view of a subsequent holder in good faith, it is a more or less inevitable consequence of the fact that the chose in action, represented by the share certificate, derives its existence and validity from its origin within the company. Attention is also drawn to the Forged Transfers Act 1891 which gives a company power to make compensation by a cash payment out of its funds for any loss arising from a transfer of any of its shares, stock, or securities, in pursuance of a forged instrument or of a transfer under a forged power of attorney.

1 *Ruben v Great Fingall Consolidated* [1906] AC 439, HL.

4.32 For the purpose of providing such compensation any company may borrow on the security of its property[1]. Where a company compensates a person under this Act for any loss arising from forgery, the company shall, without prejudice to any other rights or remedies, have the same rights and remedies against the person liable for the loss as the person compensated would have had[2].

1 CA 1985, s 1(3).
2 CA 1985, s 1(5).

4.33 The Forged Transfers Act 1892 clarifies the 1891 Act by declaring that where the shares, stock, or securities of a company have by amalgamation or otherwise become the shares, stock, or securities of another company, the last-mentioned company shall have the same power under the Forged Transfers Act, 1891, and this Act, as the original company would have had if it had continued in existence.

Completing the sale

4.34 An unpaid vendor of shares who remains the registered holder of the shares after the contract for sale retains, vis-a-vis the purchaser, the prima facie right to vote in respect of those shares[1]. This must be regarded as an exception to the principle mentioned earlier that the vendor would be obliged to vote the shares in accordance with the purchaser's instructions. Such an obligation cannot arise until the shares have been paid for.

1 *Musselwhite v CH Musselwhite & Son Ltd* [1962] Ch 964, [1962] 1 All ER 201, ChD.

4.35 In some cases questions have arisen whether a sale is effectively completed by the execution of transfer documentation which appears to be incomplete in some respect. An example is *Fitch Lovell Ltd v IRC*[1]. The appellant company made an offer to acquire shares offering to issue in exchange its own shares. The shareholders, to whom the offer and accompanying documents were sent, were thereby invited to sign a form of acceptance and a form of transfer, but not to insert in the latter the consideration, the date, or the name of the transferee. The offer was conditional on acceptance by 90% of the shareholders and later became unconditional. Allotment letters were issued by the appellant company and the shareholders' transfers and share certificates, or letters of authority to receive such certificates, were delivered to the appellant company.

1 [1962] 3 All ER 685, [1962] 1 WLR 1325, ChD.

4.36 It was held that, although the transfers signed by the shareholders to whom the offer had been made were not completed by insertion of the names of transferees, yet there had been, in the circumstances of the case, completion of the sale to the appellant company of the ordinary shares for which the offer was made by such documents as were intended by the purchaser (the appellant company) and the vendor shareholders.

4.37 Some caution is needed in understanding and applying *Fitch Lovell*. It is a stamp duty case, in which the question was whether the transfer instruments, not bearing the names of the proposed transferees, were properly to be regarded as 'conveyances or transfers on sale' within Sch 1 to the Stamp Act 1891, and it is this question which the court answered in the affirmative. It does not follow that a transfer without the name of the transferee is effective for other purposes. In particular it does not follow that it relieves the transferor of the rights and obligations of membership of the company.

Renouncable letters of allotment

4.38 Where shares are issued under renouncable letters of allotment, the effect is to vest ownership in the allottee, subject to the possibility of subsequent transfer to a third party[1].

1 *Pye-Smith v IRC* [1958] 2 All ER 785, [1958] 1 WLR 905, ChD.

SHAREHOLDER AGREEMENTS[1] AND SHARE TRANSFERS

4.39 The previous section considered the position where restrictions on transfers are contained in the articles. However, it is also possible to have such provisions in a shareholder agreement. This technique obtains the main advantages associated with putting any matter of corporate management in a Shareholder Agreement, namely that it is possible to have such an agreement without involving all the shareholders, the agreement need not be made public and the difficult arguments surrounding the enforceability of the statutory contract in s 14 of the CA 1985 have no application to such an agreement. On the other hand, they also have the disadvantages associated with shareholder agreements, namely that they bind only the parties – not the company and not any shareholders who are outside the agreement. Thus, it is in effect possible for a shareholder to transfer shares in defiance of a shareholder agreement.

1 For Shareholder agreements generally see Steadman and Jones *Shareholder Agreements*.

4.40 Where the transfer has already taken place before the other parties to the shareholder agreement discover what is going on, they have no ground to impugn the transfer, since it is *res inter alios acta*. Where they discover in advance what is proposed, it might be possible for them to obtain an injunction to restrain the transfer as being something which induces a breach of the shareholder agreement. However, the granting of the injunction is of course discretionary, and a court might well take the view that this is a case where damages will be an adequate remedy.

Share certificates

4.41 Section 182 of the CA 1985 declares shares to be personal, rather than real, property[1]. It also declares that they can be transferred in any manner laid down in the company's articles[2]. However, the provisions of the Stock Transfer Act 1963[3] override this, so that securities to which that Act applies can always be transferred by the procedure which that Act provides.

1 CA 1985, s 182(1).
2 CA 1985, s 182(2).
3 For the Stock Transfer Act 1963 see para 4.1.

4.42 Section 183 of the CA 1985 deals with transfers and registration. Companies are forbidden to register a transfer of shares unless they have received a proper instrument of transfer of the transfer is exempt under the Stock Transfer Act 1982[1], or the shares have been transferred to the new owner by operation of law[2]. A transfer may be made by the personal representative of a deceased shareholder, although that person is not the owner of the shares[3], and an application for the registration of a transfer may be made by either the transferor or the transferee[4] (the provisions of s 183(1) apply identically in either case). Where a company refuses to register a transfer of shares (assuming that it has power in its articles to do so) it must give notice of this fact to the transferee within two months of the date on which the transfer is lodged with it[5]. Failure to comply is an offence carrying a fine and a daily default fine[6].

1 CA 1985, s 183(1).
2 CA 1985, s 183(2).
3 CA 1985, s 183(3).
4 CA 1985, s 183(4).
5 CA 1985, s 183(5).
6 CA 1985, s 183(6).

4.43 Section 184 of the CA 1985 deals with certification of transfers. Where a company certifies a transfer instrument in relation to shares, this is treated as a representation by the company to any person acting on the faith of the certification that there have been produced to the company such documents as on their face show that the transferor has a prima facie title to the shares named in the transfer instrument. However, the representation goes no further than this limited statement, for s 184(1) goes on to provide that the certification is not to be taken as a representation that the transferor has any title to the shares. Section 184(2) provides that the company is liable to a person who has acted on the faith of a false certification, and that the liability is the same whether the false certification was given negligently or fraudulently. Section 184(3) provides further interpretative guidance. An instrument of transfer is deemed certificated if it bears the words 'certificate lodged' or words to the like effect.

4.44 The certification of an instrument of transfer is deemed made by a company if the person issuing the instrument is a person authorised to issue certificated instruments of transfer on behalf of the company and the certification is signed by a person authorised to certificate transfers on the company's behalf or by an officer or servant of the company or of a body corporate so authorised. A certification is deemed signed by a person if it purports to be authenticated by his signature or initials (whether handwritten or not) and it is not shown that the signature or initials were placed there neither by himself nor by a person authorised to use the signature or initials for the purpose of certificating transfers on the company's behalf.

4.45 The effect of s 184 of the CA 1985 is somewhat puzzling. From the point of view of those seeking to rely on certification, it might be thought that the most important point would be the ability to rely on the apparent authority of the person signing the certificate, since in many cases it will not be at all obvious to a reasonable outsider whether that person has actual authority or not. However, the wording of the section clearly contemplates that only actual authority will suffice. As against that, the person relying on the certificate is given at least some protection where the certificate bears the name of a person with actual authority. In such a case the certificate may be relied upon without further enquiry as to whether it was in fact issued by that person, though the company will be able to escape liability if it is able to prove that the name was used by someone else not authorised to do so. Even this escape may be of limited value however, at any rate if the person wrongfully issuing the certificate is an employee of the company. This draws attention to another uncertainty surrounding s 184.

4.46 There may be cases, such as that just mentioned, where at common law a company would be likely to be held to have made a false representation in relation to a certification and thus to be liable to anyone who had reasonably and foreseeably relied upon it. However, such a case might not fall within the wording of the CA 1985, s 184. It is unclear whether in these circumstances the company would be liable. On one view there should be liability, since nothing in s 184 is expressed as excluding or limiting the operation of any relevant common law rule. As against that, it might be observed that s 184 appears a somewhat unnecessary section unless it provides an exhaustive list of the cases where there can be liability. It seems likely that the answer lies in the history of the section.

4.47 Section 184 of the CA 1985 was formerly s 79 of the Companies Act 1948, and in 1948 the law on liability for economic loss caused by negligent misrepresentation was much more restrictive than it is at the present day. Thus, s 79 probably did extend liability when originally passed, though it has been overtaken by subsequent changes in the common law. On this basis it might be reasonable to conclude that it does not limit liability to the cases which s 184 mentions.

4.48 Section 185 of the CA 1985 deals with the duty of the company to issue share certificates. Section 185(1) requires the company, within two months of the date of any allotment of shares or of the date on which a transfer of shares is lodged with the company, to complete and have ready for delivery the certificates of all shares involved. In relation to allotments the requirement may be excluded by the terms of the issue[1].

1 CA 1985, s 185(1).

4.49 So far as transfers are concerned the requirement applies only to transfers in due form and otherwise valid, which the company is not minded to refuse to register[1] (in the latter event it would of course have to give notice of refusal within the two month period: see above).

1 CA 1985, s 185(2).

4.50 There is a further exception from the operation of CA 1985, s 185(1) in cases where the shares are transferred to a person who, under s 3 of the Stock Transfer Act 1982[1] is not entitled to a certificate or other document evidencing title to the shares[2]. However, if that person subsequently becomes entitled to such a document and notifies the company of that fact in writing, then it must be provided within two months of the date on which he gives the notice.

1 See para 4.1.
2 CA 1985, s 185(3).

4.51 Section 185(4) of the CA 1985 deals with the special position of clearing houses and nominees. Where shares of a company are allotted to a recognised clearing house or to a nominee (so designated by the rules of the relevant institution) of a recognised clearing house[1] or investment exchange, or where an application for transfer is lodged with such a party, that party is not therefore required to comply with s 185(1).

1 As defined in the Financial Services Act 1986: CA 1985, s 185(4).

4.52 Failure to comply with CA 1985, s 185(1) is an offence carrying a fine and a daily default fine[1]. A person entitled to a certificate under s 185(1) may in the event of default by the company serve a notice on it requiring it to remedy the deficiency[2]. If the company does not do so within ten days of receiving the notice, the court may, on an application from the person entitled, order the company to remedy the breach and may make a costs order personally against the company or any officer of it responsible for the breach[3].

1 CA 1985, s 185(5).
2 CA 1985, s 185(6).
3 CA 1985, s 185(7).

FINANCIAL ASSISTANCE FOR PURCHASE OF OWN SHARES

4.53 The major rules relating to this subject are contained in Part V, Chapter VI of the CA 1985 (ss 151–158). The rules may be regarded as being supplementary to those restricting a company's freedom to acquire its own shares, since the giving of financial assistance is capable of being a disguised return of the company's capital to actual or potential shareholders. However, the rules on this subject are widely regarded as excessively complex, constituting a trap for the unwary, without being drafted so as to fulfil the legitimate objectives underlying the legislation.

The basic prohibition

Section 151 restates the basic prohibition on such assistance[1]

4.54 'Subject to the following provisions of this Chapter, where a person is acquiring or is proposing to acquire shares in a company, it is not lawful for the company or any of its subsidiaries to give financial assistance directly or indirectly for the purpose of that acquisition before or at the same time as the acquisition takes place.'

1 CA 1985, s 151(1).

Section 151(2) extends the prohibition to discharges of previously incurred liabilities

4.55 'Subject to those provisions, where a person has acquired shares in a company and any liability has been incurred (by that or any other person), for the purposes of that acquisition, it is not lawful for the company or any of its subsidiaries to give financial assistance directly or indirectly for the purpose of reducing or discharging the liability so incurred.'

4.56 Financial assistance is defined in CA 1985, s 152(1):

(a) financial assistance given by way of gift;

(b) financial assistance given by way of guarantee, security or indemnity, other than an indemnity in respect of the indemnifier's own neglect of default, or by way of release or waiver;

(c) financial assistance given by way of loan or any other agreement under which any of the obligations of the person giving the assistance are to be fulfilled at a time when in accordance with the agreement any obligation on another party to the agreement remains unfulfilled, or by way of the novation of, or the assignment of rights arising under, a loan or such other agreement; or

(d) any other financial assistance given by a company the net assets of which are thereby reduced to a material extent, or which has no net assets.

4.57 The net assets are the aggregates of assets less liabilities[1].

1 CA 1985, s 152(2).

4.58 There may be financial assistance which does not involve a reduction in net assets if the recipient of the assistance is in debt to the company, so that the assistance can be transferred between one account and another, or if the assistance is funded out of the proceeds of an issue of fresh shares.

Meaning of financial assistance

4.59 In *Charterhouse Investment Trust Ltd v Tempest Diesels Ltd*[1] Templeman J observed that CA 1985, s 151 contains no technical definition of the phrase the 'giving of financial assistance', which therefore had to be interpreted in the light of the language of ordinary commerce. The commercial realities of each transaction would have to be examined to determine if it could be properly described as involving the giving of financial assistance.

1 [1986] BCLC 1, 1 BCC 99, 544.

4.60 The fact that a company received a fair value in connection with a particular transaction in the sense that any cash paid out was replaced by an asset of equivalent value did not entail that the transaction could not constitute the giving of financial assistance, as if the dominant purpose was to put the other party in funds to purchase the company's shares then the section would be contravened. But where there was no question of cash being provided, the only way in which a party could be said to have given financial assistance, was if it made a net transfer of value which reduced the price the purchaser had to pay for the shares, compared with what he would have had to pay for them if the whole transaction had not taken place.

4.61 In *British and Commonwealth Holdings plc v Barclays Bank plc*[1] a scheme of arrangement was entered into by the defendant company, the major shareholder, C Ltd, and the plaintiff banks in order to convert C Ltd's ordinary shareholding into redeemable preference shares to be redeemed by the company in four tranches. The scheme was approved by the court under s 425 of the CA 1985. As part of the arrangement, the company covenanted with the plaintiff banks to conduct its affairs so as to maintain certain asset rates and to indemnify the banks against any loss or expense incurred by the banks as a result of any breach by the company of its covenants. Pursuant to the sanction of the court, the parties further entered into an option agreement, which provided that if the company failed to redeem any of the shares, C Ltd was to be granted an option to require T Ltd to purchase the shares at the redemption price, such purchase being guaranteed and funded by the plaintiff banks. The company went into administration having failed to redeem all the shares, and C Ltd exercised its right to have the shares purchased by T Ltd. The banks and T Ltd brought proceedings against the company claiming, inter alia, damages for breach of contract and a declaration that they were entitled to an indemnity.

1 [1996] 1 All ER 381, [1996] 1 WLR 1, CA.

4.62 In answer to a preliminary special question the judge ruled that the company was not protected from liability because the agreement was unlawful under s 151(1) of the CA 1985, on the basis that the covenants in the option agreement constituted unlawful financial assistance by the company for the acquisition of its own shares by way of indemnity.

4.63 The Court of Appeal upheld this view, saying that in order for a company to be liable under s 152(1)(a)(ii) of the CA 1985 for providing unlawful financial assistance for the purchase of its shares by way of indemnity, the indemnity in question had to give assistance of a financial nature for the purpose of the acquisition of the shares. The fact that there was a contract under which a party might recover the same amount by way of damages as he would have recovered under an indemnity was not sufficient to convert that contract into an indemnity. In the circumstances, the covenants in the option agreement were bona fide covenants, the purpose of which was to reassure C Ltd and the performance of which did not involve the giving of any financial assistance. The fact that breach of the covenants might render the company liable to damages did not mean that the company gave financial assistance thereby. It followed that the option agreement did not amount to financial assistance for the purpose of the acquisition of the shares and accordingly s 151 of the CA 1985 did not preclude the company's liability.

4.64 Section 151 of the CA 1985 is the successor (with amendments) of s 54 of the Companies Act 1948. Under that section the following have been held to be prohibited:

(a) a loan made by a company to finance the borrower's purchase of shares in the company: *Selangor United Rubber Estates Ltd v Craddock (a bankrupt) (No 3)* [1968] 1 WLR 1555;

(b) a purchaser undertaking a liability (to a third party) as part of the consideration for the shares, but failing to discharge that liability, or causing the company to discharge it: *Wallersteiner v Moir* [1974] 1 WLR 991;

(c) a purchase by a company of assets at an inflated price to enable the vendor of the assets to buy shares in the company: *Belmont Finance Corpn Ltd v Williams Furniture Ltd (No 2)* [1980] 1 All ER 393;

(d) company making a payment to the vendor of the shares as an inducement to him to enter into the contract with the purchaser, even though the purchaser paid full market value out of his own resources: *Armour Hick Northern Ltd v Armour Trust Ltd* [1980] 3 All ER 833;

(e) provision of security by a company to cover a loan: *Carney v Herbert* [1985] AC 301, PC (though in that case it was held that the assistance actually given was lawful).

Despite the change in the statutory wording it is thought that all these schemes would contravene CA 1985, s 151.

4.65 The consequences of breaching the prohibition are set out in CA 1985, s 151(3): if a company acts in contravention of this section, it is liable to a fine, and every officer of it who is in default is liable to imprisonment or a fine, or both. In addition, the contract for the assistance is void and unenforceable: *Selangor United Rubber Estates Ltd v Craddock*, above, as is any guarantee supporting that contract: *Heald v O'Connor* [1971] 1 WLR. 497.

4.66 The directors responsible can be sued for breach of trust: *Steen v Law* [1964] AC 287, PC. There may also be an action in the tort of conspiracy: *Belmont Finance Corpn v Williams Furniture Ltd*, above. It is unclear whether any action lies against any third parties who might be involved. It is thought that they would have to know of the illegality, or at least be reckless as to it: *Belmont Finance*.

4.67 The effect of the illegality on the contract for the purchase of the shares is unclear. The company will not normally be a party to that contract, so any wrong-doing by it is irrelevant, but the recipient of the assistance will be a party. There are two issues here:

(a) whether the contract is enforceable while still executory;

(b) whether a purported transfer of the shares under the agreement is valid.

South Western Mineral Water Co v Ashmore suggests that the answers are: (a) No (b) Yes. The case does not however resolve the point definitively. There are conflicting overseas authorities.

4.68 An important case on the meaning of financial assistance is *Parlett v Guppys (Bridport) Ltd*[1]. In this case the plaintiff was the chairman and managing director of the defendant company (Bridport) and of three other family companies, including Guppys Properties Ltd (Properties) and Guppys Estates Ltd (Estates), in which he, his wife and his two sons each held shares. In 1988 the plaintiff agreed that in return for the companies providing him for the remainder of his service with a salary plus a profit-related bonus and a pension on his retirement, he would transfer his shares in Estates, which had been incorporated in October 1987, into the joint names of himself and his sons. It was agreed by the companies that the cost of the salary, bonus and pension would be met between them but the shares in which they would contribute to the cost were not preordained. In 1991, following his resignation as managing director of the companies, the plaintiff handed signed blank transfer forms in respect of his shares in Estates to his sons and later in the same year they nominated Bridport as the transferee of those shares and completed the transfer accordingly.

1 [1996] 2 BCLC 34, [1996] BCC 299, CA, Civil Division.

4.69 The plaintiff issued proceedings against Bridport and his sons, claiming that they had not fully honoured the agreement. The sons resisted the claim, contending that under the 1988 agreement Estates had given them financial assistance for the purpose of acquiring its shares and that the agreement was therefore unenforceable, the statutory authorisation procedures not having been followed.

4.70 The Court of Appeal held that the 1988 agreement did not have to be performed in breach of CA 1985, s 151(1), since at the date it was made there was no necessity for Estates to contribute to the cost of the plaintiff's salary, bonus and pension. It could only reasonably have been assumed that Bridport and Properties between them would be able to bear the whole of such cost. The directors of those companies could, therefore, reasonably and prudently have made provision for the whole of that cost to be borne by the companies, and in discharge of their contractual and statutory duties to the plaintiff and Estates they were bound to do so. On that footing there was no reduction in the net assets of Estates and no financial assistance within s 151(1). It followed that the 1988 agreement was valid and enforceable[1].

1 See also *Brady v Brady* [1989] AC 755, [1988] 2 All ER 617, HL; *Carney v Herbert* [1985] AC 301, [1985] 1 All ER 438, PC; *Lawlor v Gray* [1979] CA Transcript 409; *United Dominions Corpn (Jamaica) Ltd v Shoucair* [1969] 1 AC 340, [1968] 2 All ER 904, PC; *Re John Willment (Ashford) Ltd* [1979] 2 All ER 615, [1980] 1 WLR 73.

4.71 Two points may be made about *Parlett*. The first is that the use of the other family companies (ie other than Estates) as a way of circumventing the statutory prohibition is possible only because the various companies are not members of a group. The second is that the Court of Appeal shows a distinct (and understandable) distaste for allowing the defendants to rely on CA 1985, s 151 as a way of escaping from an agreement freely entered into. It is of course questionable whether it would have been legitimate to assume that the assistance was provided by companies other than Estates if it had appeared that Estates was the only company with any significant assets.

The larger purpose exception

4.72 Section 153(1), (2) of the CA 1985 provide an exception to the prohibition laid down by CA 1985, s 151. The exception applies where the company's principal purpose in giving the assistance is not to give it for the purpose of that acquisition, or where the giving of assistance for that purpose is merely an incidental part of some larger purpose of the company and the assistance is given in good faith in the interests of the company.

4.73 This provides an exception from the prohibition of CA 1985, s 151(1). There is a similar exception from s 151(2). This applies to assistance given after the acquisition of the shares, ie assistance which reduces or discharges any liability already entered into. The conditions for the exception are the same as those in s 153(2).

4.74 In both subsections of CA 1985, s 153 there are two distinct exceptions, but it seems that there is little or no practical difference between them. The section is somewhat difficult to construe for two reasons. First, the test is in large measure a subjective one, since it depends upon the company's perception of the purpose of giving the assistance. Second, deciding whether there is some larger purpose also involves a considerable element of judgement. There is apparently no reported case in which it has been held that assistance which would otherwise have been unlawful is saved by the larger purpose exception.

4.75 A rare case in which the exception was considered is *Brady v Brady*[1]. The first plaintiff and first defendant, who were brothers, carried on a family business through B Ltd and a number of subsidiary companies, one of which was jointly owned by the second plaintiff and the second defendant, both of whom were sons of the first defendant. Two principal activities were carried on: a road haulage business and the manufacture and distribution of drinks. The brothers quarrelled and the resulting deadlock put the existence of the business in jeopardy.

1 [1989] AC 755, [1988] 2 All ER 617, HL.

4.76 The first plaintiff petitioned under what is now s 459 of the CA 1985 for an order to buy out the first defendant or for the company to be wound up. After negotiation, however, an agreement was reached whereby the business would be split up so that one brother would acquire the haulage business and the other the drinks business. The agreement provided for a scheme of corporate reorganisation whereby the assets of the business were divided equally but the main company was left in existence. The defendants later took the view that the assets had not been equally divided and they refused to complete the transaction. The plaintiffs commenced an action for specific performance. The defendants argued[1] that the agreement had been illegal on the grounds that the proposed arrangements constituted the giving by B Ltd of financial assistance in connection with the purchase of its own shares, contrary to s 151(1), (2) of the CA 1985.

1 Other arguments put forward by the defendants are not considered here, having no relevance to share capital questions.

4.77 At first instance it was held that the principal purpose of the giving of the financial assistance was not to reduce or discharge any liability incurred by any person for the purpose of the acquisition of the shares, but was incidental to the larger purpose of the arrangement and fell within the larger purpose exception.

4.78 The Court of Appeal was divided. O'Connor LJ held that the assistance had not been given in good faith in the interests of the company, since it involved (in his view) one company giving away some of its assets, a proceeding which could never be in the interests of the company. Nourse LJ held that the scheme was ultra vires the powers in the company's memorandum, so that the issue of CA 1985, s 151 did not arise. He observed, however, that in his view the scheme would also have failed under s 151. Though he also suggested, tentatively, that it might have been saved by the larger purpose exception. Croom-Johnson LJ dissented in the result, holding that the scheme was both intra vires and in the best interests of the company.

4.79 In this unsatisfactory and confusing state of affairs the matter reached the House of Lords, which held that the financial assistance had not been an incidental part of some larger purpose of the company within CA 1985, s 153(2)(a) and therefore, prima facie, it did not fall within the exception to the prohibition in s 151 of the CA 1985 against a company giving financial assistance for the acquisition of its own shares[1].

1 However, the House of Lords went on to hold that the assistance could lawfully be given out of distributable profits.

4.80 Lord Oliver, giving the only substantial speech, held that the scheme was intra vires and could be justified as being in the best interests of the company. The difficulty arose in relation to the larger purpose exception. Lord Oliver traced the history of the provision, which first appeared in s 42 of the Companies Act 1981, possibly for the purpose of dispelling the doubt raised in *Belmont Finance Corpn Ltd v Williams Furniture Ltd (No 2)*[1] as to whether a transaction entered into partly for the genuine commercial purposes of the company and partly to put the purchaser in funds to complete the transaction was caught by the prohibition. However, the word 'purpose' is ambiguous.

1 [1980] 1 All ER 393, CA.

4.81 Section 153(2)(a) of the CA 1985 contemplates at least two possible situations. The first is where there is a principal purpose and a subsidiary purpose (as in *Belmont Finance*), and it is necessary to enquire which is which. If the principal purpose is to relieve the purchaser of the shares from his indebtedness, then the exception cannot apply. The second situation is where it is clear that the purpose of the assistance is to reduce the indebtedness, but that reduction is merely incidental to some larger purpose such as a commercially sensible reconstruction (as in *Brady*).

4.82 In Lord Oliver's view it is not acceptable to apply CA 1985, s 153(2)(a) to the second situation, though it may apply to the first. This conclusion is reached by distinguishing between the purpose for which the assistance is given and the reason why that purpose is formed. In the second example Lord Oliver's analysis would be that the purpose of the assistance is to reduce the indebtedness, though the reason for forming that purpose is the desire to effect the reconstruction. As Lord Oliver observed, the acquisition of the shares was not merely an incident of the scheme – it was the essence of the scheme, and for this reason the larger purpose exception cannot apply.

4.83 The reasoning deployed in this case is convoluted, though ultimately logically convincing. The major problem to which it gives rise is that it leaves very little scope for the larger purpose exception to operate. Arguably this conforms to what was intended by the legislature. Certainly it is true, as Lord Oliver also observes, that in interpreting the exception one should have regard to the reasons for the prohibition on financial assistance and should consider whether the assistance in question appears to be within the mischief at which the rules are aimed. It cannot be doubted that the assistance given in *Brady* does fall within the mischief. It would seem to follow that it should be permitted, if at all, only subject to the substantive and procedural safeguards laid down by the CA 1985, ss 155 ff.

Other exceptions

4.84 Section 153(3), (4) of the CA 1985 provide further miscellaneous exceptions to s 151, as follows:

Section 153(3)

- A distribution by way of lawful dividend, or in the course of a winding up.
- The allotment of bonus shares.
- A reduction of capital confirmed by order of the court under CA 1985, s 137.
- A redemption or purchase of redeemable shares, made in accordance with CA 1985, ss 159–181.
- Anything done in pursuance of an order of the court under s 425 of the CA 1985 (compromises and arrangements with members and creditors).
- Anything done under an arrangement made in pursuance of s 110 of the Insolvency Act 1986 (acceptance of shares by liquidator in winding up as consideration for sale of property).
- Anything done under an arrangement made between a company and its creditors which is binding on the creditors by virtue of Part I of the Insolvency Act 1986.
- These are all procedures which are subject to other forms of regulation within the Companies Acts, and in some cases also to the sanction of the court. For this reason they are excluded from the prohibition of the financial assistance rules.

Section 153(4)

- Where the lending of money is part of the ordinary business of the company, the lending of money by the company in the ordinary course of its business.
- The provision by a company, in good faith in the interests of the company, of financial assistance for the purposes of an employees' share scheme.
- The provision of financial assistance in connection with steps taken to facilitate share transactions between present or past employees and/or their spouses or minor children.
- The making by a company of loans to persons other than directors employed in good faith by the company with a view to enabling those persons to acquire fully paid shares in the company, or its holding company, to be held by them by way of beneficial ownership.

4.85 These are cases where it might be thought that the mischief of the financial assistance rules does not arise, since transactions falling within these categories should not be regarded as amounting to a disguised use of the company's capital to assist the purchase of shares.

Public companies

4.86 In the case of public companies s 154 of the CA 1985 imposes an additional restriction on the giving of assistance under s 153(4) (but not on the giving of assistance under s 153(3)). It is that the company must have net assets, which are not reduced by the giving of the assistance, or, to the extent that those assets are thereby reduced, the assistance must be given out of distributable profits.

4.87 'Distributable profits' has the same meaning as in Part VIII of the CA 1985, ie accumulated realised profits less accumulated realised losses[1]. This is the definition used for determining which profits may properly be distributed by way of dividend.

1 CA 1985, s 263(3).

Relaxation of section 151 for private companies

4.88 Sections 155–158 of the CA 1985 deal with the circumstances in which private companies may give financial assistance in connection with the purchase of shares in the company notwithstanding the prohibition in s 151.

Source of funds

4.89 Either the company must have net assets, which are not reduced by the giving of the assistance, or the funds must be provided from distributable profits[1].

1 CA 1985, s 155(2).

Groups of companies

4.90 Section 155 of the CA 1985 does not permit the giving of assistance by a subsidiary for the acquisition of shares in the holding company if the company is also the subsidiary of a public limited company, which is itself the subsidiary of the holding company.

4.91 Consider the following group structures:

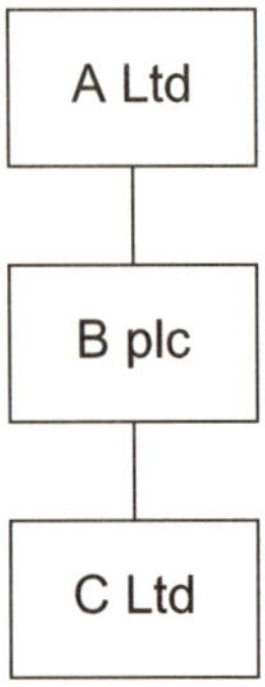

C Ltd may not give assistance for the purchase of shares in A Ltd.

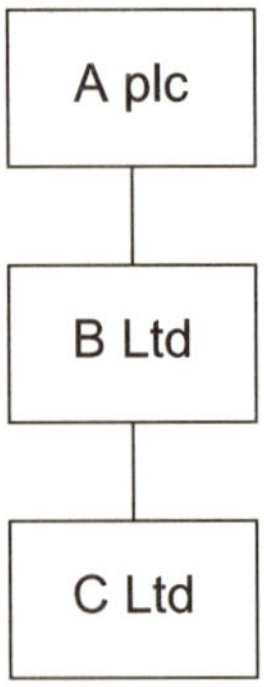

C Ltd may give assistance for the purchase of shares in B Ltd. Section 155 of the CA 1985 does not prohibit it from giving assistance for the purchase of shares in A plc, though s 153 may do so.

Requirement of approval

4.92 Unless the company which is to give the assistance is a wholly-owned subsidiary, the giving of assistance must be approved by a special resolution of the company in general meeting[1].

1 CA 1985, s 155(4).

4.93 Where the assistance is given by a subsidiary for the acquisition of shares in its holding company, the assistance must be approved by the company giving it, the holding company and any intermediate holding company. Thus, in the second example above A plc, B Ltd and C Ltd must all give their approval.

4.94 However, the above rule does not apply to wholly owned subsidiaries. Thus, if either B Ltd or C Ltd is wholly owned, no special resolution is needed. The special resolution is needed if either is not wholly owned.

4.95 The special resolution must be passed on or within one week after the date on which the directors make the special resolution required by CA 1985, s 155[1]. In most cases the meeting will be an Extraordinary General Meeting, which will require 14 days notice. The content of the resolution must be shown in the notice, together with the fact that it is being proposed as a special resolution. Short notice procedure is available, provided that the necessary majority of members consents.

1 CA 1985, s 157(1).

4.96 Persons holding at least 10% of the shares (10% of the members in a company not limited by shares) may petition the court for the cancellation of the resolution, provided that they have not voted for the resolution or consented to it[1].

1 CA 1985, s 157(3).

4.97 The procedures and powers of the court when such an application is made are the same as those for an objection to the re-registration of a public company as private under ss 53 and 54 of the CA 1985[1].

1 CA 1985, s 157(3).

4.98 The statutory declaration made by the directors, together with the auditors' report annexed to it, must be available for the inspection of members at the meeting where the resolution is passed. Failure to comply with this requirement renders the resolution ineffective[1].

1 CA 1985, s 157(4).

Requirement of statutory declaration

4.99 The directors of the company giving the assistance are required to make a statutory declaration in respect of that assistance. Where the assistance is given in connection with the purchase of shares in the company's holding company, a similar declaration must be made by the directors of the holding company and of any intermediate holding company[1].

1 CA 1985, s 155(6).

4.100 The statutory declaration must give particulars of the assistance to be given and of the nature of the company's business, and must identify the person to whom the assistance is to be given[1]. An important case on this provision is *Re SH & Co (Realisations) 1990 Ltd*[2]. There was no doubt in this case that financial assistance was given, and a statutory declaration was made in an effort to comply with s 156 of the CA 1985. It was argued that the charge was not enforceable because the particulars of the charge were not sufficiently comprehensive to satisfy the statutory requirement in s 156(1). In particular, it was argued that the particulars were defective because they failed to identify:

(a) the property subject to the charge;

(b) the kind of charge (ie fixed or floating); or

(c) the guarantee given in connection with the charge.

1 CA 1985, s 156(1).
2 [1993] BCLC 1309, [1993] BCC 60 (Companies Court), ChD.

4.101 Counsel for the unsecured creditors, in seeking to argue that there had not been compliance with the statutory requirements, produced a specimen completed form of prescribed particulars for the two boxes, showing how it should be done. The first box of that draft referred not just to the grant of the debenture, but also to the agreement to pay, the guarantee and the grant of fixed and floating charges over its assets. The specimen box of principal terms contained similar information as to the creation of various charges over various items of property and assets.

4.102 It was submitted that the reference to the grant of a 'debenture' in the box for principal terms was insufficient to constitute the necessary particulars. This is because the word 'debenture' has no precise meaning beyond referring to a document which either creates or acknowledges a debt[1].

1 *Knightsbridge Estates Trust Ltd v Byrne* [1940] AC 613 at 621–622, [1940] 2 All ER 401 at 405–406 per Viscount Maugham. Section 744 of the Companies Act 1985 defines 'debenture' as including: 'debenture stock, bonds and any other securities of a company, whether constituting a charge on the assets of the Company or not.'

4.103 It was also submitted that the use of the word 'security' in the box for principal terms did not necessarily mean that a charge had been created by the debenture.

4.104 As there were no particulars in the statutory declaration showing the property charged, the kind of charge or the giving of the guarantee, the declaration did not reveal the nature and extent of the financial assistance to be given. A person looking at the statutory declaration available for inspection at Companies House would not be in a position to make an assessment of the impact on the company of the financial assistance given. The fact that a person could find that information elsewhere, such as in the Charges Register kept at the Companies Registry, did not constitute an excuse for failing to comply with the requirements for the contents of the statutory declaration.

4.105 The result is that there has been no compliance with CA 1985, s 155(6). The general prohibition on financial assistance in s 151 of the CA 1985 has been infringed and the security granted by, and the covenants in, the debenture are unenforceable.

4.106 Mummery J rejected these arguments. He observed that it is of course important that there should be compliance with procedures prescribed by Parliament for the protection of the interests of those dealing with or concerned in a company, whether they be creditors or shareholders. It is common ground in this case that the statutory declaration was completed in good faith by an experienced firm of solicitors, acting on behalf of the directors, in an honest attempt to ensure compliance with the statutory requirements. Those facts would not, however, constitute an excuse for non-compliance. The duty is to comply with the objective requirements, not simply to use best endeavours to comply with them. Here, there had been compliance, though it could not be doubted that the case fell close to the line.

4.107 The legislation does not in terms state how detailed the particulars must be. As a matter of ordinary English, 'particulars' consist of details, items or points of information[1]. The legislation simply limits the scope of particulars to be contained in the statutory declaration to:

> '... such particulars of the financial assistance to be given, and of the business of the company of which they are directors, as may be prescribed and shall identify the person to whom the assistance is to be given.'

The question is, therefore, how detailed, how particularised, do those particulars have to be to comply with the prescribed form? In answering that question, the court should have two particular factors in mind.

1 *Royal Bank of Canada v IRC* [1972] Ch 665 at 675, [1972] 1 All ER 225 at 232 per Megarry J.

4.108 First, the principal purpose of requiring a statutory declaration is to ensure that financial assistance provided by a private company satisfies the criteria in CA 1985, s 156(2). The statutory declaration may at the same time provide information to those who search the company file at Companies House where the statutory declaration and auditors' report have been delivered pursuant to s 156(5).

4.109 But it is not the principal purpose of the statutory declaration to provide, for example, particulars of the property charged or the kind of charge. There is no requirement for registration of the declaration by the Registrar. The requirement is simply for delivery of the declaration to the Registrar.

4.110 Second, the consequences of non-compliance are severe. It is not simply a question of making the security and covenant for payment unenforceable, though those are serious matters in themselves. Penalties are incurred under CA 1985, s 156(6) and, more seriously, under CA 1985, s 151(3).

4.111 Following an approach similar to that adopted by Megarry J in *De Courcy v Clement*[1], the judge concluded that the matters omitted from the particulars about the identity of the property charged, the kind of charge granted, and of the guarantee, do not prevent the particulars in fact contained in the declaration from being reasonably and fairly described as particulars of the form and principal terms of financial assistance.

1 [1971] Ch 693 at 698–699, [1971] 1 All ER 681 at 685.

4.112 The judge went on to offer advice to solicitors preparing documentation of this kind. They should err on the side of caution and include the fuller form of particulars as exemplified by counsel's specimen form. Particulars in that form would remove any possible doubt as to whether there had been compliance.

4.113 The declaration must also state that in the directors' opinion the company will be able to pay its debts immediately after the assistance is given and that the company will be able to pay its debts as they fall due during the year immediately following the giving of the assistance. In the rare case where it is proposed to commence the winding up of the company within the next 12 months, the requirement is that the company will be able to pay its debts within 12 months of the commencement of the winding up[1].

1 CA 1985, s 156(2).

4.114 In forming their opinion the directors must take account of the same liabilities (including contingent and prospective liabilities) as would be relevant under s 122 of the Insolvency Act 1986 to the question whether the company is able to pay its debts[1]. These factors are set out in s 123 of the Insolvency Act 1986, and the most important are:

(a) debt of at least £750 not paid within three weeks of service of statutory demand;

(b) execution of judgment against company returned unsatisfied, in whole or in part, proved to the satisfaction of the court that the company is unable to pay its debts as they fall due; or

(c) liabilities exceed assets.

1 CA 1985, s 156(3).

4.115 It appears, however, that the test here does not work in the quite the same way as it would in s 123 of the CA 1985. In the context of that section a company which meets any of the stated tests will normally be presumed to be unable to pay its debts, but it is unlikely that the opposite applies, ie a company may be unable pay its debts even though none of these tests is satisfied. In the context of the financial assistance rules it seems that these tests are no more than guidelines, not least since the directors are concerned not merely with whether the company can at present pay its debts but also with whether it will continue to be able to do so for the next 12 months.

Auditors' report

4.116 A report from the company's auditors must be annexed to the statutory declaration. This must state that the auditors have enquired into the company's affairs and are not aware of anything to indicate that the opinion expressed by the directors as to the above matters is unreasonable[1].

1 CA 1985, s 156(4).

4.117 Note the negative phrasing and limited ambit of this report. The auditors are not required to warrant the accuracy of the directors' opinion, nor even its reasonableness: they have only to say that they see nothing to indicate positively that it is unreasonable.

Delivery of documents to Registrar of Companies

4.118 The statutory declaration and auditors' report must be delivered to the Registrar together with the special resolution. If no special resolution is required (because the company providing the assistance is a wholly-owned subsidiary) then the declaration and report must be delivered within 15 days of the making of the declaration[1].

1 CA 1985, s 156(5).

Offences

4.119 A contravention of the CA 1985, s 156(5) renders the company and every officer of it who is in default liable to a fine and, for continued contravention a daily default fine.[1]

1 CA 1985, s 156(6).

4.120 A director who makes the statutory declaration without having reasonable grounds for the opinions expressed in it is liable to imprisonment or a fine, or both[1].

1 CA 1985, s 156(7).

Timing

4.121 Where a special resolution is required the assistance shall not be given before the expiry of four weeks from the date when the resolution is passed (or the last of them in group situations where more than one special resolution is required). This allows time for dissentient shareholders to petition the court under CA 1985, s 157[1].

1 CA 1985, s 158(2).

4.122 The only exception to the above rule is found where every member of the company (or all the companies, if more than one) who was entitled to vote on the resolution voted in favour of it. In this event, the four-week waiting period does not apply.

4.123 If there is a petition by dissentient shareholders, then the giving of the assistance is postponed until the final determination of the petition, unless the court orders otherwise[1].

1 CA 1985, s 158(3).

4.124 The latest time for the giving of the assistance is eight weeks from the making of the statutory declaration (or, if more than one, from the making of the earliest of the statutory declarations)[1].

1 CA 1985, s 158(4).

4.125 Note that the earliest available time is measured from the passing of the resolutions, whereas the latest possible time is measured from the making of the declarations. Also, the relevant declaration is the earliest one, whereas the relevant resolution is the latest one. In cases involving several companies, careful attention to timing is needed, or it is possible to get into a situation where compliance with all the rules is impossible! However, even in these circumstances relief is at hand as a result of the decision in *Re NL Electrical Ltd, Ghosh v 3i plc*[1]. 3i plc provided financial assistance for the acquisition of shares in a company. The directors made a statutory declaration as required by s 155(6) of the CA 1985 but did so on a form which was not then, but which had been, the prescribed form. The statutory declaration was delivered to the Registrar of Companies about one month after it had been made by the directors.

1 [1994] 1 BCLC 22 (Companies Court), ChD.

4.126 The question arose as to whether (a) the failure to use the correct prescribed form, or (b) the failure to deliver the statutory declaration of the director within the 15 days as required by s 156(5) of the CA 1985 rendered the financial assistance illegal. It was held that the financial assistance had been lawfully given.

4.127 The obligation of the directors under s 155(6) of the CA 1985 is to make the statutory declaration in the prescribed form and not on a prescribed form. Since all the required particulars were delivered to the Registrar the fact that a particular form was not used did not entail that there had been non-compliance with the statutory obligation to deliver the prescribed particulars. Moreover, the failure to deliver the particulars within the 15 days as required by CA 1985, s 156(5) did not result in the financial assistance being improperly provided.

4.128 The only consequence of failing to deliver the particulars within the 15-day period was a breach by the company to comply with its statutory duty under CA 1985, s 155(6). Presumably, although the case does not say so, this breach of duty might be actionable by anyone who could show that he had suffered loss arising from it. Of course it is hard to imagine how such a situation could arise. A more difficult question arising from this approach is to what extent compliance with other requirements of the financial assistance procedure is essential in order to render the assistance lawful.

Foreign companies and financial assistance

4.129 In *Arab Bank plc v Mercantile Holdings Ltd*[1] the plaintiff bank granted a loan facility to the second defendant for the express purpose of enabling it to acquire the share capital of Q Ltd, the parent company of the first defendant Q Ltd and the second defendant were both incorporated in England and registered under the English Companies Acts. The first defendant was incorporated in Gibraltar, but it maintained a place of business in Great Britain and was an 'oversea company' and a 'subsidiary' of Q Ltd for the purposes of the CA 1985 but was not itself a 'company' for the purposes of that Act. Subsequently, the bank wished to exercise remedies under the loan. The defendants contended, inter alia, that the bank's security was void as having been granted in contravention of s 151(3) of the CA 1985, which prohibited a company or any of its subsidiaries from giving financial assistance for the purpose of the acquisition of its shares. It was accepted that if the first defendant had been incorporated in England and registered under the English Companies Acts the security provided by it to the bank would have constituted the unlawful giving of financial assistance.

1 [1994] Ch 71, [1994] 2 All ER 74, ChD.

4.130 The questions arose whether s 151 of the CA 1985 made it unlawful for a foreign subsidiary of an English parent company to give financial assistance for the purpose of the acquisition of shares in the parent company, and whether the mere giving of such assistance by the foreign subsidiary also constituted the unlawful giving of financial assistance by the parent company contrary to s 151. Both questions were answered in the negative. Section 151 of the CA 1985 was not intended to have extra-territorial effect (there being no indication to the contrary in the section), so the term 'any of its subsidiaries' in s 151 was to be construed as limited to those subsidiary companies which were English companies. Accordingly, s 151 did not prohibit a foreign subsidiary of an English parent company from giving financial assistance for the purpose of the acquisition of shares in its parent company. Moreover, the mere giving of financial assistance by the subsidiary did not ipso facto constitute the unlawful giving of financial assistance by the parent company contrary to s 151 of the CA 1985, since the prohibition was directed to the assisting company, not to its parent company.

EQUITABLE ASSIGNMENTS OF SHARES

4.131 Equitable assignments of shares are very commonly encountered. They are used as a way of raising money on shares (since mortgages of personal property are normally thought to be impossible). They are also encountered in many savings schemes where shares are bought for the benefit of savers with the intention that the saver should have the beneficial entitlement to the shares. The possible difficulties arising from this situation were considered in *Re Harvard*

Securities Ltd[1]. The company had bought a number of shares for client and had become the registered holder of those shares. When the company went into liquidatio, the question arose whether it held the shares on trust for the clients who were shown in its books as the registered holders. It was held that it did, since in relation to shares there can be a trust of an undivided part of a parcel[2], although it is established that this is not possible in relation to chattels[3].

1 [1997] 2 BCLC 369 Neuberger J.
2 See also *Hunter v Moss* [1994] 3 All ER 215, [1994] 1 WLR 452, CA.
3 *Re Wait* [1927] 1 Ch 606, CA; *Re London Wine Co (Shippers) Ltd* [1986] PCC 121 Oliver J; *Re Stapylton Fletcher Ltd* [1995] 1 All ER 192, [1994] 1 WLR 1181 Judge Baker QC; *Re Goldcorp Exchange Ltd (in receivership)* [1995] 1 AC 74, [1994] 2 All ER 806, PC.

TRANSMISSION OF SHARES

4.132 The term 'transmission' in relation to shares refer to the process by which the title to shares is transferred on the death of the registered holder. The topic requires to be treated separately because the legal rules and procedures are to some extent different from those applying to a transfer inter vivos. On the death of a person, title to his property normally vests in his personal representatives, but this rule cannot operate in a straightforward way in the case of shares because of the rule that the share register is decisive of the legal title to shares. The beneficial interest in the shares will go to the persons entitled to the estate, though of course the next step is often to realise the value of the shares by selling them.

MORTGAGES OF SHARES

4.133 Where shares are mortgaged, questions may arise about the remedies to be exercised by the mortgagee in the even of default on the loan. The courts are reluctant to accept attempts by the mortgagee to cut down his common law dury to deal properly with the shares. In *Bishop v Bonham*[1] the charge agreement provided that on the defendant's failure to repay the loan the plaintiff would be entitled to sell the shares in such manner, upon such terms and for such consideration as he 'may think fit', and he would not be liable for any loss 'howsoever arising' in connection with the sale; and that the defendant would at the plaintiff's request execute a transfer vesting the legal title to the shares in the purchaser. The defendant did not repay the loan and, when the plaintiff sold the shares at a price regarded by the defendant as an undervalue, the defendant refused to execute a transfer in favour of the purchaser. The plaintiff claimed specific performance of the applications for summary judgment and an order striking out the defendant's defence and counterclaim.

1 [1988] 1 WLR 742, [1988] BCLC 656, CA.

4.134 The Court of Appeal held that under the general law there was a duty on a mortgagee to take reasonable care to obtain a proper price when exercising his power of sale; that on its true construction the charge agreement authorised the plaintiff to sell the shares in such manner, upon such terms and for such consideration as he might think fit, within the limits of the duty of care imposed by the general law, so that he was not exempted from liability for loss arising from a failure to take reasonable care to obtain a proper price.

4.135 Another question arising in relation to charges on shares is that of priority of charges. In *Champagne Perrier-Jouet SA v HH Finch Ltd*[1] the articles of association prohibited the company from granting a loan on the security of its shares and gave the company a first and paramount lien on any shares registered in the name of any person indebted to the company. Clause 12 provided that if moneys were presently payable, the company might sell any shares on which the company had a lien in such manner as its directors thought fit and, by clause 13, the directors could authorise some person to transfer such shares to a purchaser and the shares were thereafter to be registered in the name of the purchaser. There was also a general restriction on the transferability of the shares. A director of the defendant company who held a substantial number of its shares, was indebted to the company as a result of the company paying a number of his bills and supplying him with wines for a company under his control. The moneys owing were recorded in a 'loan account' and he undertook to repay his indebtedness to the defendant company at a rate of not less than £52 a year. Later he gave the plaintiffs a guarantee for the debts and liabilities incurred by the other company to the plaintiffs and he also mortgaged his shares in the defendant company as security by depositing the share certificates. Subsequently he failed to make the £52 payment under the deed, and the company obtained judgment against him for the full sum outstanding.

1 [1982] 3 All ER 713, [1982] 1 WLR 1359.

4.136 On the plaintiffs' claim for a declaration that their rights under the mortgage took effect in priority over any rights the defendant company had to a lien over his shares or, alternatively, for declarations as to the respective rights of the plaintiffs and the company over the shares, it was held that the indebtedness of the director to the defendant company, not being for moneys lent for a time and to be returned in money's worth, was not a loan and, therefore, there was no prohibition under the articles against the company having a lien on the director's shares for the sums he owed the company. It was also held that, notwithstanding that the deed considerably deferred the payment of the director's indebtedness to the company, the defendant company had a lien over his shares from the date his indebtedness to the company arose and that, accordingly, the company's lien had priority over the plaintiffs' equitable charge.

4.137 It was further held that the defendant company had no need to apply to the court for authority to sell the shares in exercise of its lien since its directors might authorise some person to transfer the shares to a purchaser on behalf of a shareholder; that if a person was nominated, he could both initiate and complete the transaction on behalf of the director but that, on the true construction of the articles, the company's power to sell the shares did not override the provisions restricting transferability of the shares to existing shareholders and the transfer had to be made in accordance with the provisions of that article and, therefore, the defendant company could not sell the shares on the open market for a higher price than they could obtain from an offer to the existing shareholders.

Chapter 5

Removing capital

5.1 The principles underlying the doctrine of capital maintenance were discussed in Chapter 1, where it was also mentioned that in recent years company law has departed from the strict doctrine by allowing the removal of a company's capital in some circumstances. These circumstances are considered in the present Chapter. Buy-back of shares is now allowed under ss 159–181 of the CA 1985, whilst reductions of capital under what are now ss 135 ff of the same Act have a much longer history[1].

1 CA 1985, ss 135–141 were CA 1948, ss 66–71.

COMPANY BUY-BACK OF OWN SHARES

5.2 Sections 159–181 of the CA 1985 deal with company buy-back of own shares. Section 159 allows for the issue of redeemable shares, though at any given time a company must have some shares which are not redeemable within the meaning of this section. It is important to understand that redeemable shares in this context are shares which the company is entitled to redeem at its option and irrespective of the wishes of the shareholder.

5.3 A company (the acquiring company) is not precluded by s 143 of the CA 1985, or under the rule in *Trevor v Whitworth*[1], from acquiring the shares of another company (the acquired company) in circumstances where the sole asset of the acquired company is shares in the acquiring company[2]. This rule is a simple application of the principle of corporate personality, since the acquiring company will own the shares of the acquired company, but will not own the acquired company's property. Of course, there may be a different problem if the acquired company thereby becomes a subsidiary of the acquiring company, since the subsidiary is forbidden to hold shares in its parent company[3], though as is argued in Chapter 1, the provisions of s 23 of the CA 1985 do not appear to be drafted so as to catch this case.

1 (1887) 12 App Cas 409, [1886–90] All ER Rep 46.
2 *Acatos & Hutcheson plc v Watson* [1995] 1 BCLC 218, [1995] BCC 446.
3 CA 1985, s 23.

5.4 Public companies must redeem shares out of the proceeds of a fresh issue of shares or out of distributable profits[1]. For the different rules for private companies see below.

1 CA 1985, s 160.

5.5 Redeemed shares are treated as cancelled, and this reduces the issued capital but not the authorised capital[1].

1 CA 1985, s 160.

5.6 Even where shares have not been issued as redeemable shares within the meaning of CA 1985, s 159 they may still be repurchased by the company if the articles so authorise[1] and the rules in ss 159–161 apply to such a repurchase except that the manner of the repurchase need not be determined by the articles[2].

1 CA 1985, s 162.
2 CA 1985, s 162(2).

5.7 There are further special rules relating to both market and off-market purchases of the shares of public companies.

5.8 The fact of the repurchase must be declared to the Registrar of Companies on the prescribed form within 28 days of being made[1].

1 CA 1985, s 169.

5.9 An agreement to repurchase shares is not specifically enforceable against the company, nor does breach of it by the company give rise to an action for damages[1]. In *British and Commonwealth Holdings plc v Barclays Bank plc*[2] a scheme of arrangement was entered into by the defendant company, the major shareholder, C Ltd, and the plaintiff banks in order to convert C Ltd's ordinary shareholding into redeemable preference shares to be redeemed by the company in four tranches. The scheme was approved by the court under s 425 of the CA 1985. As part of the arrangement, the company covenanted with the plaintiff banks to conduct its affairs so as to maintain certain asset rates and to indemnify the banks against any loss or expense incurred by the banks as a result of any breach by the company of its covenants. Pursuant to the sanction of the court, the parties further entered into an option agreement, which provided that if the company failed to redeem any of the shares, C Ltd was to be granted an option to require T Ltd to purchase the shares at the redemption price, such purchase being guaranteed and funded by the plaintiff banks. The company went into administration having failed to redeem all the shares, and C Ltd exercised its right to have the shares purchased by T Ltd. The banks and T Ltd brought proceedings against the company claiming, inter alia, damages for breach of contract and a declaration that they were entitled to an indemnity.

1 CA 1985, s 178.
2 [1996] 1 All ER 381, [1996] 1 WLR 1, CA.

5.10 In answer to a preliminary special question, the judge ruled that the company was not protected from liability by virtue of CA 1985, s 178(2)[1].

1 For other points in the case see Chapter 3.

5.11 The Court of Appeal upheld this view, saying that in deciding whether a company was excused liability to pay damages pursuant to s 178(2) of the CA 1985, the court had to ask itself whether there had been a failure to redeem and, if so, whether the claimed damages were in respect of that failure, in the sense of being damages recoverable because of the failure to redeem; a loose connection or relationship was not sufficient. On the facts, the damages claimed by the banks and T Ltd were in respect of breaches of covenants in the option agreement and not in respect of the failure to redeem, and accordingly the company was not excluded from liability by s 178(2)[1].

1 See also *Howe v David Brown Tractors (Retail) Ltd (Rustons Engineering Co Ltd, third party)* [1991] 4 All ER 30, CA.

5.12 In *Vision Express (UK) Ltd v Wilson*[1] the plaintiff company sued D an ex-employee, alleging various breaches of duty while he was employed by them. As part of the settlement of the action an order was made which required, inter alia, that P Co purchase D's shares and share options in P, which he had obtained as part of an employee share scheme. The question arose whether this order could be enforced, given that P was trying to purchase its own shares and that the requirements of CA 1985, ss 143 ff apparently could not be satisfied. P argued that s 143 did not apply to orders made in settlement of an action, at least where the company had a strong case that it was entitled to the shares. It was held, that s 143 does apply to such cases, since it is not alleged that the company has a proprietary right in the shares, ie there is no doubt that the scheme is that the company *purchases* the shares. Presumably the position might be otherwise if for some reason the company were asserting a proprietary (even equitable) right to the shares.

1 [1995] 2 BCLC 419.

Special rules for private companies

5.13 Private companies may alternatively redeem shares out of capital if so authorised by their articles[1].

1 CA 1985, s 171.

5.14 The transaction must also be approved by special resolution[1]. The directors must make a statutory declaration that the company is thereupon able to pay its debts and, so far as can be foreseen, will remain able to do so for the next year[2]. This must be supported by an auditors' report stating that they have enquired into the company's affairs, that the proposed capital payment has been properly calculated and that they can see nothing to suggest that the directors' opinion is unreasonable in all the circumstances.

1 CA 1985, s 173(2).
2 CA 1985, s 173(3).

5.15 The special resolution must be passed within one week of the making of the declaration and the payment out of capital must be made between five and seven weeks after the date of the Resolution[1]. Holders of shares to be redeemed must not vote on the proposal[2].

1 CA 1985, s 174(1).
2 CA 1985, s 174(2).

5.16 The proposal must be advertised in a national newspaper and in the Gazette[1] and any member or creditor may object to the proposal within five weeks of the resolution having been passed in which case the court may approve the proposal, with or without modifications, or may reject it[2].

1 CA 1985, s 176.
2 CA 1985, s 177.

5.17 The CA 1985 gives no guidance on the criteria to be adopted in considering whether to approve or reject a contested proposal for redeeming shares out of capital. There appears to be no reported case on the subject, which leaves the need to try to articulate some principles which are likely to lead to satisfactory results. It is suggested that the most promising approach to this problem is to reason by analogy with other cases where changes in the structure of the company's share capital are subject to consideration by the court on an objection by an interested party. The best known examples are objections to alterations of class rights under CA 1985, s 127[1] and, perhaps a closer analogy, objections to reductions of share capital under s 136[2]. For present purposes it is sufficient to note that the court needs to take into account the principles underlying the notion of capital maintenance, the most important of which may be said to be the protection of creditors.

1 See Chapter 3.
2 See para **5.24** below.

5.18 Clearly, the statutory procedures which must be followed before there can be any question of buy-back are to some extent designed to offer that protection, so the role of the court in this respect must be limited. Nevertheless, it is possible that there would be cases where the letter of the statutory provisions was complied with, yet there was a risk of undue prejudice to creditors. Such cases should, however, be rare, since the directors of the company should have considered the question of the financial stability of the company before deciding to enter into the transaction.

5.19 A secondary consideration taken into account by the courts in deciding on reduction of capital applications under CA 1985, s 136 is the possible prejudice to shareholders. This will have to mean shareholders other than those whose shares are to be bought back, and other than any who voted in favour of the resolution to authorise the buy-back. However, it is not clear how such shareholders are likely to be prejudiced, except to the extent, if any, that they can argue that the financial stability of the company is impaired by the buy-back. This argument is exactly the same as that which might be made by the creditors and would therefore appear to give rise to the very same issues.

CAPITAL REDUCTION

5.20 Sections 135–138 of the CA 1985 deal with reduction of capital by a company. What is being considered here is reduction in any way. In particular, s 135(1) sets out three ways of effecting the reduction. These are:

(a) extinguishing or reducing liability on any of its share in respect of share capital not paid-up;

(b) cancelling paid-up share capital which is lost or unrepresented by available assets (either with or without extinguishing or reducing liability on any of its shares);

(c) paying off any paid-up share capital which is in excess of the company's wants (either with or without extinguishing or reducing liability on any of its shares).

5.21 Section 135(2) of the CA 1985 also contains a necessary consequential power for the company to alter its memorandum by reducing the amount of its share capital and its shares accordingly.

Section 135

5.22 The three limbs of CA 1985, s 135 are likely to be used in somewhat different situations. Numbers 1 and 3 arise most naturally where the company has surplus cash (especially 3). Number 1 may also sometimes be used where it has become clear that a particular allottee is not going to be able to pay for his shares in full. Number 2, by contrast, is normally a sign that the company is in financial difficulty, or at least that it has suffered significant losses. Adherence to the principle behind it may be regarded as no more than the practical implementation of the rule that the share capital is supposed to represent a permanent fund available to creditors. Thus the amount shown standing to the credit of the share capital account in the balance sheet ought properly to be reduced once it is clear that the assets in question no longer exist. The artificialities of this doctrine in modern company law have already been criticised, though it is also quite clear from reading the statutory provisions dealt with in this book that the Companies Acts do still reflect that doctrine in a great many places.

5.23 Section 136 of the CA 1985 allows a company which has passed a special resolution for reducing its capital to apply to the court for an order confirming that reduction[1]. Although this provision is expressed in permissive rather than mandatory terms, the logic of this area of the law is obviously that the reduction cannot have effect until it is confirmed by the court, so that the application for confirmation is in effect mandatory. If this were not so, then a company would have no incentive to apply for confirmation. Given the creditor protection provisions which operate in the case of an application for confirmation (discussed below) this would clearly be an unacceptable state of affairs.

1 CA 1985, s 136(1).

5.24 Section 136 of the CA 1985 applies to applications for orders confirming a reduction of capital. It applies automatically in any case where the proposed reduction of capital involves a diminution of liability in respect of unpaid share capital or the repayment to a shareholder of any paid-up share capital, as well as to any other where the court directs that it shall apply. The reason for applying these provisions in these circumstances is that they are cases in which the protection notionally afforded to creditors by the presence of the company's paid-up capital (or at least the liability of shareholders for calls on unpaid capital) is weakened by the elimination of part of the capital or the liability, as the case may be.

5.25 However, CA 1985, s 136(6) also gives the court power to direct that these provisions shall not apply, notwithstanding that the proposed reduction does involve either reduction of liability for unpaid capital or repayment of paid-up capital. Such a direction may be made generally or in respect of particular classes of creditors, but apparently not in relation to individual creditors. Presumably this is on the basis that the way to deal with individual creditors is to dispense with their consent under s 136(5), though it must be noted that this does not by any means produce the same result as excluding them from the consent procedure in the first place. The latter means that the company is not required to provide for their claims, whereas the former means that some provision will be needed.

5.26 Where CA 1985, s 136 applies, s 136(3), (4) and (5) give creditors certain rights. Section 136(3) allows creditors to objection to the reduction of capital if, at the date fixed by the court, they are entitled to any debt or claim which would be admissible against the company on a winding up. Section 136(4) requires the court to settle a list of creditors entitled to object to the proposed reduction. For that purpose it must ascertain the names of those creditors and the amount of their debts or claims, though this must be done without requiring an application from any creditor[1]. Then the court may (but apparently is not required to) publish notices fixing a time within which creditors not entered on the list are to claim to be so entered, on pain of being excluded from the right to object to the proposed reduction.

1 CA 1985, s 136(4)(a).

5.27 Once the list of creditors has been finalised, the court must consider whether to approve the reduction in capital, taking due account of any objections which might be raised by creditors. Section 136(5) of the CA 1985 allows the court to approve the proposal even though one or more creditors might object. It does this using the rather curious form of words that the court may 'dispense with' the consent of particular creditors. However, this power to dispense with the consent of creditors is available only where the company either provides for the full amount of the debt or claim or provides an amount fixed by the court on the same basis as would apply if the company were in the process of being wound up by the court. The latter option will be appropriate where there is a dispute about the amount of the debt or where the debt is for some reason contingent or unascertained, so that it is not yet possible to fix its amount with precision. No doubt in practice the prospect of the court conducting an enquiry and fixing an amount to be provided in respect of the debt will often lead companies and their creditors to come to some out of court agreement about the treatment of the debt, in return for which the creditor will not object to the reduction.

5.28 Section 137 of the CA 1985 gives the court power to make an order confirming the reduction. Before doing so it must be satisfied that every creditor who is entitled to object to the reduction either has in fact consented or has had suitable provision made for his claim. It is very important to note that this is mandatory. The drafting of the section does not permit the court to override the objections of a creditor unless adequate provision has been made for his debt, or unless he is a member of a class of creditors in relation to whom there has been a direction that the objection provisions are not to apply. Once the position of all creditors has been adequately dealt with, the court has a discretion, but not a duty to make an order confirming the reduction. Section 137(1) also expressly declares that the order may be subject to such terms and conditions as the court thinks fit.

5.29 Section 137(2) of the CA 1985 gives the court further powers when making an order confirming a reduction of capital. First, it may make an order requiring the company to add to its name for a specified period the words 'and reduced' as the last part of its name[1]. Second, it may require the company to publish, in whatever form the court directs, the reasons for the reduction of capital or such other information in regard to it as the court thinks expedient, with a view to giving proper information to the public[2].

1 CA 1985, s 137(2)(a).
2 CA 1985, s 137(2)(b).

5.30 Section 138 of the CA 1985 deals with the registration of the order for reduction. The company must produce to the Registrar the order confirming the reduction, together with a minute approved by the court and showing the company's new share capital arrangements, ie the amount of the share capital, the number of shares into which it is divided, and the amount (if any) which at the date of the registration is deemed to be paid up on each share. The first two of these cannot of course subsequently be varied without going through one of the statutory procedures for the alteration of capital[1]. The third item, the amount paid up on each share (which could of course differ from share to share if some are fully paid and others are not) could subsequently be varied without using any of the statutory procedures if amounts outstanding on individual shares are later paid-up.

1 That alteration could of course as well be an increase as a reduction.

5.31 Section 138(2) of the CA 1985 provides that on registration of the order and minute, but not before, the resolution for reducing share capital takes effect. Notice of the registration is to be published in such manner as the court may direct[1]. The Registrar is required to certify the registration of the order and minute. The certificate must be either signed by the Registrar or authenticated by his official seal[2]. It is conclusive evidence that all the requirements of the Act, with regard to the reduction of share capital, have been complied with and that the company's share capital is as stated in the minute. This effectively draws a line under the history of the company's share capital at that point. Thus s 138(5) provides that the minute, when registered, is substituted for the capital clause is the company's memorandum. It is valid and alterable as if it had originally been contained therein (though this cannot possibly mean that the lateration has any retrospective effect). This substitution is regarded as an alteration of the memorandum for the purposes of s 20 of the CA 1985, which requires the memorandum to be updated when alterations are made and requires, on pain of a fine, that copies of the memorandum issued after the alteration shall embody the alteration.

1 CA 1985, s 138(2).
2 CA 1985, s 138(4)(a).

5.32 Section 139 of the CA 1985 deals with the special case of a public company which seeks to reduce its capital below the authorised minimum for a public company[1]. Perhaps surprisingly, the CA 1985, ss 135–138 do not forbid a public company to seek to do this, nor do they forbid the court to grant such an application. However, where the effect of a confirmed resolution for reduction of capital is to bring the capital of a public company below the authorised minimum, the Registrar must not register the order under s 138 unless the court so directs or the company is first re-registered as a private company.

1 Currently £50,000: CA 1985, s 117.

5.33 It is very hard to imagine circumstances in which the court would order the registration of the order even though the company had not been re-registered as a private company. It would clearly be quite unacceptable for the company to continue in business as a public company without having the necessary capital. Thus, the only possible situation would appear to be where the company is proposing to re-register as a private company, but has not yet done so. Even here however, it would appear that the obvious answer to a request for registration of the resolution is that the company should first put its house in order by completing re-registration. Indeed, a public company which seeks to reduce its capital below the authorised minimum must know that re-registration is an inevitable consequence, and the two procedures ought properly to proceed in tandem.

5.34 There is a further good answer to any suggestion that registration of the capital reduction should be allowed with re-registration of the company as private. Section 139(3) of the CA 1985 allows the court to authorise re-registration without the need to pass the special resolution normally required for this purpose under s 53. Although this power is expressed in general terms, its presence in s 139 leads one to suppose that it should only be exercised in cases where there is an urgent need for the re-registration and where that urgency results directly from the fact of a reduction in capital. Where the court makes an order for this purpose, it must specify in the order the alterations in the company's memorandum and articles to be made in connection with the re-registration[1].

1 CA 1985, s 139(3).

5.35 Once the court has made such an order, the company may then be re-registered as a private company, if an application in the prescribed form and signed by a director or the secretary of the company is delivered to the Registrar, together with a printed copy of the memorandum and articles as altered by the order[1]. On receiving such an application, the Registrar retains it and the other documents delivered with it, and issues the company with a new certificate of incorporation in the form appropriate to a private company[2]. At that point the company becomes a private company and the alterations to the memorandum and articles set out in the court's order take effect[3]. The certificate is conclusive evidence that the requirements of CA 1985, s 139 in respect of re-registration have been complied with, and that the company is a private company.

1 CA 1985, s 139(4).
2 CA 1985, s 139(5).
3 CA 1985, s 139(5)(a).

5.36 Section 140 of the CA 1985 deals with the liability of members on reduced shares. Where a company's share capital is reduced, the liability of members (including for these purposes any contributory) is correspondingly reduced. The point is of course relevant only in relation to shares which are not fully paid-up. Section 140(1) provides for the recalculation of outstanding liabilities as the difference between the amount of the share as fixed by the minute and the amount (if any) deemed to have been paid-up on it.

5.37 Two points need to be made about CA 1985, s 140(1). First, the reference to the amount of the share cannot be interpreted as meaning simply the nominal value of the share. There may be cases where the original issue price involved a substantial premium. In the case of a private company[1] there is no requirement that the premium be paid-up on issue. A possible effect of the reduction of capital would be that the premium is reduced but not eliminated. In such a case the only possible interpretation of the reference in s 140(1) is that it means the issue price of the shares (including premium) less whatever reduction has been made by the approved reduction in capital.

1 For the different position in a public company see CA 1985, s 117.

5.38 The second point about CA 1985, s 140(1) relates to the amount which is deemed to have been paid on the share. One possible provision of an order confirming the reduction of capital is to reduce also the amount deemed to have been paid-up on shares. This may be done so as to reduce the prejudice to creditors arising from the loss of capital. It effectively transfers the burden of the loss of capital from the creditors to the shareholders, who remain liable to contribute to the company's capital. Of course it cannot automatically be assumed that the reduction in the amount deemed paid on each share will be exactly proportionate to the reduction in capital: it would be perfectly possible to spread the burden of the reduction in capital between creditors and shareholders by making a less than proportionate reduction. There would, however, seem be no case for ever making a more than proportionate reduction.

5.39 The remaining provisions of CA 1985, s 140 apply in the case where a creditor who has the benefit of a debt or claim against the company is not entered on the list of creditors, either because the proceedings for the reduction of the company's capital do not come to his notice or because he does not know their nature and effect with respect to his claim and, after the reduction of capital the company is unable to pay his claim within the meaning of s 123 of the Insolvency Act 1986.

5.40 This reference to s 123 of the Insolvency Act 1986 is somewhat obscure, given that the test is not whether the company at that point is able to pay its debts generally, but specifically whether it is able to pay this creditor's claim. It is easy enough to see that the requirement will be satisfied where the company as a whole is insolvent, but where it is not insolvent (but is in financial difficulties) the position is less clear. It is suggested that the best interpretation of this provision is that the requirement will be considered to be satisfied if a statutory demand has been served and is not paid within the statutory period of 21 days. Of course this potentially renders the company liable to compulsory winding up by the court (provided that the debt in question is at least £750[1]) but s 140 of the CA 1985 appears to afford a different remedy, and one which is available whatever the level of the debt.

1 IA 1986, s 123.

5.41 Section 140(3) of the CA 1985 provides that every person who was a member of the company at the date of the registration of the order and minute under CA 1985, s 138 is liable to contribute to the debt an amount not exceeding the amount which he would have been liable to contribute if the company had begun to be wound up on the day before the registration of the order and minute. The effect of this is that the liability of any member in relation to partly paid shares is determined as if the reduction had not taken place; thus, any reduction in the amount deemed to be outstanding on the shares will not benefit shareholders in relation to a claim falling within this provision. An odd side-effect of this is that a creditor who is missed from the official list of creditors, or who can plead ignorance of the nature and effect of the proceedings, is likely to be in a better position than one who has a proper involvement in the original proceedings, since he may obtain additional rights against shareholders personally. What is especially surprising about this provision is its inclusion within the scope of its protection of the shareholder whose claim is really based on ignorance. This seems a most unusual departure from the normal principle that everyone is deemed to know the law.

5.42 Section 140(4) of the CA 1985 continues the principle of s 140(3) into cases where the company is in fact wound up. However, it does not give the creditor any automatic right to claim. Rather, it gives the court a discretion, if the circumstances of s 140(2) are established, to settle a list of contributories and then to make and enforce orders for payment against such people as if they were ordinary contributories in a winding up. Section 140(5) goes on to provide that s 140 is not to affect the rights of the contributories inter se.

5.43 Finally in this area, s 141 of the CA 1985 creates a regulatory offence for any officer of a company who wilfully conceals the name of a creditor entitled to object to a reduction of capital or wilfully misrepresents the nature or amount of any debt owing to a creditor or aids, abets or is privy to any such concealment or misrepresentation.

5.44 Section 142 of the CA 1985 deals with the situation where the net assets of a public company are found to be not more than half of its called-up share capital. Section 142(1) imposes an obligation on the directors to convene an Extraordinary General Meeting of the company. The meeting must be called not later than 28 days from the date on which the situation is first known to any director of the company and must be held not more than 56 days from that date. The subsection says that the purpose of the meeting is to consider whether any, and if so, what, steps should be taken to deal with the situation. Although this section appears under the general heading 'Maintenance of Capital' it is to be observed that nothing in the section requires the company to take any steps to deal with the situation – it is sufficient for the meeting to consider the possibility of taking steps and then to decide against it. Obviously, in such circumstances it would be incumbent on the directors to justify the inaction, since the section is certainly not intended to relieve the directors of any other duty to which they would otherwise be subject. Presumably it is assumed that in a s 142 situation, the directors will always be looking to take action. Whilst this assumption is very probably true, it does rather undermine the rationale of the section.

5.45 Competent directors are likely to want to take action well before the company reaches the fairly dire situation envisaged by CA 1985, s 142, so it is unlikely that the section will have much relevance for them. Moreover, the action they take will not in most cases include the calling of an Extraordinary General Meeting – there seems little point in making the company's difficulties public, nor in consulting with shareholders, who may well not have much to offer in the way of sensible advice. Any shareholder whose opinion the directors did value could usefully be consulted informally, which is likely to be more constructive that a set-piece Extraordinary General Meeting.

5.46 It is hard to avoid the conclusion that CA 1985, s 142 has really very little do with the maintenance of capital, though it may have a certain amount to do with respecting the rights of shareholders. Be that as it may, s 142(2) creates regulatory offences, punishable by fine, for any director of the company who knowingly and wilfully permits or authorises a failure to convene a meeting within the statutory 28 days and/or a continuing failure to summon a meeting after the end of the 28-day period.

5.47 Section 142(3) of the CA 1985 restricts the business of a meeting convened in pursuance of s 142 by providing that no matter may be considered at such a meeting which could not have been considered at that meeting in the absence of s 142(1). Once again the wording is opaque. However, leaving aside the fact that in most cases the meeting would not have been convened in the absence of s 142(1), s 142(3) appears to mean that the ordinary requirements as to notice of particular types of resolution[1] continue to apply – the apparent urgency of the situation is not allowed to override these rules.

1 CA 1985, ss 378, 379.

5.48 The statutory rules are couched in broad discretionary terms, and it is necessary to look at the case law in order to understand what is in practice likely to happen. The modern practice appears to be that reductions which have been through all the necessary procedures are almost always confirmed. The basic principle is still that stated by Harman J in *Re Ratners Group plc*[1]. Three conditions must be satisfied if the court is to ratify a reduction. These are:

(a) all shareholders must be treated equitably (which appears to mean equally unless they have consented to be treated less than equally);

(b) the proposals must have been fairly explained to and put before the shareholders at the general meeting, so that their consent can properly be regarded as an informed consent;

(c) creditors of the company must be safeguarded so that money cannot be applied in any way which is detrimental to them.

Where these conditions are met, the reduction is more or less certain to be confirmed. Other cases, discussed below, touch on other peripheral points in the exercise of the discretion.

1 [1988] BCLC 685, 4 BCC 293; earlier cases in this area include *Scottish Insurance Corpn Ltd v Wilsons and Clyde Coal Co Ltd* [1949] AC 462, [1949] 1 All ER 1068, HL; *Thomas de la Rue & Co* [1911] 2 Ch 361 Eve J; *Welsbach Incandescent Gas Light Co* [1904] 1 Ch 87, CA; and see Farrar *Company Law* (4th edn, 1998) at pp219 ff.

Where loss of capital not permanent

5.49 There is case law on the position where a company has suffered a loss of capital which may or may not be permanent. In *Re Jupiter House Investments (Cambridge) Ltd*[1] the company had incurred a substantial loss on the sale of some of its property. It resolved by special resolution to write off the loss by reducing its share capital. It subsequently applied to the court for confirmation of the proposed reduction, the petition alleging that 'capital to the extent of £384,058 and upwards had been lost or was unrepresented by available assets'. Evidence filed in support of the petition showed that there was a reasonable chance of the loss being recovered through litigation so that it could not be said that the loss was permanent.

1 [1985] 1 WLR 975, [1985] BCLC 222, ChD.

5.50 In order to safeguard the interests of creditors which might be prejudiced if money later recovered, which represented capital, was paid out as dividends, the company, inter alia, offered an undertaking to the court that any damages recovered through litigation would be placed in a permanent capital reserve which would be available, if necessary, to satisfy any of the company's creditors but would not be available for distribution as dividends to shareholders. It was held that where loss of capital was sought to be proved that loss meant permanent loss and not a temporary fall in the value of some capital asset; but that where the loss could not be proved to be permanent, but the company had given an undertaking which ensured that if the lost capital was in fact recovered it would not be distributed as dividends the court would in the exceptional circumstances confirm the proposed reduction.

5.51 A similar approach was adopted in *Re Grosvenor Press plc*[1], where the company had a deficit which it wanted to eliminate by a reduction of its share capital. The proposed reduction was not put forward as a cancellation of paid-up share capital which was lost since there was a possibility that the capital would be recovered. Instead the company offered and the Registrar accepted an undertaking that if any of the missing capital was in fact recovered it would be set aside in a special reserve so that the interests of company's existing creditors should not be prejudiced. The company sought the confirmation of the court of the proposed reduction of capital, and the court developed the approach taken in the previous case, observing that the effect of setting aside a permanent capital reserve was to safeguard the interests, not only of existing creditors but of future creditors and shareholders, and that as there were already statutory safeguards to protect the interests of future creditors and shareholders there was no need except in special circumstances for the court to require a reserve to be set aside indefinitely. The court also held that accordingly, since there were no special circumstances the proposed reduction would be confirmed on the terms of an undertaking which would protect only the interests of creditors of the company existing at the date on which the reduction of capital was to take effect.

1 [1985] 1 WLR 980, [1985] BCLC 286, ChD.

Procedural errors

5.52 In *Re Willaire Systems plc*[1] the company summoned an extraordinary general meeting to authorise the making of a rights issue and to effect a reduction of its capital. It was subsequently discovered during proceedings to obtain the court confirmation of the reduction of capital that the circular setting out the special resolution for the reduction of capital contained a number of minor inaccuracies. In particular, it stated that the number of unissued ordinary shares was 2,073,420 instead of the correct figure of 2,073,417, and it also stated the number of issued shares as 14,926,580 instead of the correct figure of 14,926,583. A shareholder sought to challenge the reduction on these grounds.

1 [1987] BCLC 67, 2 BCC 99, 311, CA.

5.53 The Court of Appeal held that where a resolution for the reduction of a company's capital contains an error, then the court has either a statutory jurisdiction under s 137 of the CA 1985, or inherent jurisdiction, to confirm the reduction on terms which corrected the error, provided the error was of such an insignificant character than no one could be thought to be prejudiced by its correction and the way in which it was to be corrected was clear. On the facts the errors in the resolution were minuscule and the court could have confirmed the original reduction of capital by correcting the errors without there being any need to summon another meeting of the shareholders to pass a corrective resolution authorising the reduction.

5.54 A case where the error was of a more significant nature is *Re European Home Products plc*[1]. The company petitioned for confirmation of the cancellation of its share premium account. The necessary resolutions approving the cancellation were passed by the shareholders without any significant opposition. The circulars sent to shareholders accompanying the notices of the meetings to approve the cancellation stated that the cancellation was designed to enable the company to write off goodwill arising from acquisitions made by the company. Goodwill of £38.5m was mistakenly stated to have arisen from the acquisitions, the true figure being £17.5m. The directors of the company were content to write off goodwill of only £17m and to increase the reserve account against which goodwill arising in future could be written off. They sent circular letters to the shareholders informing them of the mistake, their proposal and their intention to seek the court's sanction for the cancellation. Shareholders who wished to attend the court hearing were instructed to return a form to receive notification of the place and date of the hearing. None attended the hearing to oppose the conformation of the cancellation of the share premium account.

1 [1988] BCLC 690, 4 BCC 779, ChD.

5.55 The court confirmed the cancellation, but observed that as a matter of general principle it would be reluctant to confirm a resolution passed on the strength of an inaccurate circular. A heavy onus was placed on the company to show that any inaccuracy could not have influenced the minds of reasonable shareholders. Reasonable shareholders could have been, but on the facts were not, influenced by the inaccuracy.

Reductions of share premium account[1]

5.56 The issues relating to this have been considered in three reported cases. In *Re Ratners Group plc*[2] it was said that the principles on which the court will sanction a reduction of a company's share premium account are similar to those on which the court will sanction a reduction of share capital. Provided that the shareholders are treated equitably, that they have had the facts explained to them and that creditors are safeguarded, a company may reduce its capital in any way it thinks fit and the court will normally sanction the reduction.

1 For the requirement for a share premium account see Chapter 2.
2 [1988] BCLC 685, 4 BCC 293, ChD.

5.57 Where a capital reserve is to be created by the reduction of the share premium account, and that reserve is to be used to eliminate goodwill, it is irrelevant to the exercise of the court's discretion to sanction the reduction that the share premium account, and the goodwill to be eliminated, arose at the same time and in connection with the same transaction. The court will not refuse to sanction a reduction of the share premium account to make reserves available for writing off goodwill where the company has no present intention to write off goodwill, provided that the company proves that it is likely to need the reserve created to write off goodwill in the future, so that in exercising its discretion the court is not acting in vain.

5.58 In *Re Thorn EMI plc*[1] the company, which was the holding company of a group of companies, sought confirmation by the court of a reduction of its share premium account. The company had grown by acquisition and planned to make further acquisitions. It wished to have available a reserve against which to 'write-off' the goodwill which arose on the accounts of the underlying companies being consolidated and which in previous years had been 'written off' against the profit and loss account. It was held that the court had a discretion whether or not to confirm a reduction of a share premium account and would normally do so where: (a) the shareholders were treated equitably, (b) the reduction proposals were properly explained, (c) the creditors were safeguarded and (d) the reduction was for a discernible purpose.

1 [1989] BCLC 612, 4 BCC 698, ChD.

5.59 In *Re Quayle Munro Ltd, Petitioners*[1] the company applied to the court for confirmation of a cancellation of its share premium account. The main purpose of the cancellation was to write off an accrued deficit on the company's profit and loss account. As the amount of the share premium account exceeded that deficit the company lodged an undertaking:

(a) that the amount of the share premium account would be transferred to a special reserve; and

(b) that so long as any creditors at the date of the cancellation remained unpaid or did not consent, the reserve would not be treated as realised profit to write off any accrued deficit on the company's profit and loss account.

The undertaking also required the company to retain in the reserve a sum sufficient to repay certain preference shares.

1 [1994] 1 BCLC 410 Ct of Sess (First Division).

5.60 The application was remitted in accordance with Scottish procedure to a reporter. In this report he queried the use of the reserve to write off future deficits on the profit and loss account and its use to pay the preference shares since the CA 1985, especially s 171, contained detailed provisions for the purchase by a company of its own shares out of capital. It was held that the use by the company of the reserve to write off future deficits on its profit and loss account was not objectionable in principle. The company's creditors at the date of the cancellation would be protected by the undertaking. The funds in the reserve might also be treated by the company as profits available for distribution in terms of s 263(3) of the CA 1985 and could therefore be used to repay the preference shares in terms of CA 1985, s 160(1)(a). Section 171 of the CA 1985 was not relevant to a repayment of the preference shares from the reserve. Section 136(3)–(5) did not apply in this case. The cancellation would be confirmed.

Duties of shareholders

5.61 When voting on a proposed reduction of capital which also involves a variation of class rights shareholders must consider whether the proposed reduction is in the best interests of the holders of the class of share which is affected[1]. A reduction of capital which is not in accordance with class rights is nevertheless regular if it has been effectually sanctioned in accordance with the regulations of the company, provided that those holding a sufficient majority of the shares of that class voted in favour of the reduction in the bona fide belief that they were acting in the interests of the general body of members of that class; if there were such a sanction the court would confirm the reduction unless the opposition proved it to be unfair; if there were no sanction the court would only confirm the reduction if it were proved to be fair[2].

1 *Re Holders Investment Trust Ltd* [1971] 2 All ER 289, [1971] 1 WLR 583, ChD.
2 See also *Carruth v Imperial Chemical Industries Ltd* [1937] AC 707, [1937] 2 All ER 422, HL.

Exercise of the court's discretion

5.62 Some important general principles about the exercise of the court's discretion to sanction reductions of capital were laid down in *Ex p Westburn Sugar Refineries Ltd*[1]. The appellant company wished to reduce its share capital by paying off paid-up share capital which was in excess of its wants. It had formed an investment holding company, subscribed for 1000 2s. shares therein, and had provisionally agreed to transfer to it, at book value, certain shares and debentures in private companies which it held and a sum of 3% funding stock. In exchange the holding company was to pay £100 in cash and to issue to the appellant company, or its nominees, shares of 2s. each in itself credited as fully paid. The appellant company proposed to reduce its capital from £609,000, divided into 609,000 shares of £1 each, to £548,100, divided into the same number of shares of 18s. each, by returning paid-up capital to the extent of 2s. on each share, this 2s. being satisfied by the transfer to the shareholder concerned of one fully-paid 2s. share in the holding company.

1 [1951] AC 625, [1951] 1 All ER 881, HL.

5.63 The articles of the appellant company authorised the reduction of capital subject to the approval of the court, and the necessary resolutions had been passed by the company. The petition asking for the sanction of the court to the proposed reduction made it clear that the capital to be returned was in excess of the company's wants, but did not state by how much it was surplus. The value of the assets to be transferred to the holding company was considered by expert opinion to be far in excess of the book value, but these assets formed only a comparatively small part of the total assets of the appellant company, the value of the assets to be retained by the company (as shown in its last balance sheet) exceeding £1.4m while its liabilities were less than £500,000.

5.64 The House of Lords held that there was nothing in principle objectionable in achieving a reduction of capital by a reorganisation of this kind. Equally, the transfer at book value was not in principle objectionable, though in such a case it would be right for the court closely to scrutinise the facts so as to ensure that the rights of creditors of the transferor company, the shareholders, and the investing public should not be defeated or injured. In the present case the appellant company was in a strong position as regards its retained liabilities and assets and so the rights of the creditors and the interests of the shareholders, actual and prospective, were amply protected and, therefore, the proposed reduction should be confirmed[1]. How much of the paid-up share capital the company could dispense with for the future was a domestic matter which the shareholders and their managers must decide among themselves. If the amount which they had decided on worked no injustice to creditors or to shareholders, the court should not be concerned to know the precise figure by which the company's capital was surplus to its requirements.

1 See also *British and American Trustee and Finance Corpn v Couper* [1894] AC 399, HL and *Poole v National Bank of China Ltd* [1907] AC 229, HL.

5.65 It appears from the case law that the courts are in general favourably disposed to reductions of capital which have been through the statutory procedures and will not lightly uphold an objection from minority shareholders. In *Re Saltdean Estate Co Ltd*[1] preference shareholders objected to the proposed repayment of their share capital, on the ground that the company was highly profitable and that the premium which they were being offered on their shares was inadequate. It was held that the proposed reduction of capital was not unfair because the holders of the preferred shares were always at risk that such right to participate in profits might at any time be frustrated by a liquidation, or a reduction of capital, properly resolved on by a sufficient majority of the members of the company. It was also said that the proposed cancellation of the preferred shares on a reduction of capital was in accordance with the rights attached to those shares and did not involve a variation or abrogation of any such rights.

1 [1968] 3 All ER 829, [1968] 1 WLR 1844, ChD.

5.66 In *Re William Jones & Sons Ltd*[1] the memorandum of association provided that in the event of the company's being wound up and there being more than enough to repay the capital of the preference shares and the capital of the ordinary shares, the preference shareholders would be entitled to participate in the surplus assets rateably with the ordinary shareholders until they received another 25s. per share. The company passed a resolution proposing to reduce its authorised capital by returning the capital paid up on the preference shares of the company, without any premium, and cancelling those shares. The preference shares, at the time, stood at less than par and there was no prospect of the company being wound up. No class meeting of the preference shareholders had been held to approve the reduction. It was held that it was fair in all the circumstances, and in view of the fact that no one had appeared to object to the confirmation of the reduction of capital, that the court should confirm the reduction.

1 [1969] 1 All ER 913, [1969] 1 WLR 146, ChD.

5.67 It is difficult to draw any general lesson from *Re William Jones*. Certainly it is surprising to find the court confirming a reduction of capital in the absence of a class meeting. The only possible justification for this is the fact that no preference shareholder had come forward to oppose the reduction. Any who had done so would surely have had a very strong case based on the procedural irregularity. As to the substance of the matter it seems that the fairness of the proposal must rest on the fact that the preference shares then stood below par, so that the holders of those shares were getting a premium over market value. This had to be balanced against the possibility (at that time hypothetical and apparently remote) that on a winding up they might have received a premium to the par value.

Dispensing with list of creditors

5.68 In *Re Lucania Temperance Billiard Halls (London) Ltd*[1] there was a proposal to reduce capital, and the company sought the court's permission to dispense with a list of creditors. The company was the tenant of 29 leasehold properties, 21 of which were held on terms beneficial to the company and eight of which were neither beneficial nor onerous. The company had sufficient cash resources, to cover its liabilities (apart from those under the leases) as well as the amount proposed to be returned to the shareholders, with an adequate margin. This raised the general question of the circumstances in which it would be appropriate to grant such permission. It was held that the company would need to satisfy the court that, so far as could be reasonably foreseen, the relevant creditors would not be adversely affected by the proposed reduction of capital and would be no worse off than if they had attended the application and objected, in which case the court could dispense with a creditor's assent only if the company secured payment of his claim by appropriating a sufficient fund; a sufficient fund was, a fund of like amount to that which the court would fix if the company were being wound up compulsorily.

1 [1966] Ch 98, [1965] 3 All ER 879, ChD.

5.69 In the present case there were no assignees of the leases, the performance of whose obligations might be regarded as likely to relieve the tenant company from performing its obligations under the leases, with the consequence that if the assets of the company were reduced the landlords might be prejudiced; accordingly the landlord's possible objections could not be disregarded[1].

1 See also *Re House Property and Investment Co Ltd* [1954] Ch 576, [1953] 2 All ER 1525.

5.70 Although an adjudication of the amount to be provided should proceed on the footing that the company would remain in possession of the leaseholds for an indefinite period yet, where a leasehold was held for a long term, the court in the exercise of its discretion under would not normally insist on the full rent for the whole term being covered by the amount fixed, and ten years' rent would normally suffice where the lease was not onerous.

Cancelling part of a class of shares

5.71 Where the reduction takes the form of cancelling part (but not all) of a class of shares and it is not possible to obtain the consent of all the shareholders of the affected class, it has been said judicially that it is preferable to proceed by way of a scheme of arrangement under s 425 of the CA 1985, rather than by way of a reduction of capital under s 135[1].

1 *Re Robert Stephen Holdings Ltd* [1968] 1 All ER 195n, [1968] 1 WLR 522, ChD, though in that case Plowman J did nevertheless confirm the reduction.

Where reduction is achieved by cancelling unissued shares

5.72 There is no reduction of capital until an approved minute has been registered; but a resolution which diminishes share capital in a way that does not require the confirmation of the court, as, eg, a resolution for the subdivision and cancellation of unissued shares, can take effect from the time of its being passed. Accordingly, if on a reduction of capital unissued shares are to be subdivided and cancelled, the cancellation should be effected in practice as part of the process of reduction of capital and the subdivision by means of a resolution to take effect on the reduction taking effect rather than separately under s 135 of the CA 1985 notwithstanding that under s 135 the cancellation of share capital is not a reduction of capital within the Act[1].

1 *Re Castiglione, Erskine & Co Ltd* [1958] 2 All ER 455, [1958] 1 WLR 688, ChD.

Form of minute in case of reduction of share premium account

5.73 Where a reduction of share capital, including the writing down of part, or the writing off of the whole, of the share premium account is confirmed by the court, the minute approved by the court should not refer to the writing down or the writing off of the share premium account. If the share premium account is written off, such a reference is irrelevant, and if it is written down, the substitution of the minute for the corresponding part of the memorandum would give rise to a conflict between s 4 of the CA 1985 (which provides that the conditions of the memorandum cannot be altered except as expressly provided by the Act) and s 130 (which enables the share premium account to be applied in certain ways)[1].

1 *Re Paringa Mining and Exploration Co Ltd* [1957] 3 All ER 424, [1957] 1 WLR 1143, ChD.

No need to aver that the company is carrying on business

5.74 In presenting to the court a petition for approval of a reduction of capital it is not necessary to aver that the company is carrying on business[1].

1 *Re Great Universal Stores Ltd* [1960] 1 All ER 252n, [1960] 1 WLR 78, ChD, disapproving observations of Kekewich J in *Re Wallasey Brick & Land Co Ltd & Reduced* (1894), 63 LJ Ch 415, 70 LT 870; see also *British and American Trustee and Finance Corpn v Couper* [1894] AC 399, [1891–94] All ER Rep 667.

FORFEITURE AND SURRENDER OF SHARES

5.75 Forfeiture of shares most commonly occurs where shares are issued partly-paid or nil-paid and the shareholder fails to meet calls for the payment of some or all of the outstanding sums. Table A deals with the possibility of forfeiture. Regulation 12 allows the directors to make calls at any time (subject to any contrary provision in the original terms of allotment) in respect of money unpaid on the allotment of the shares. Shareholders are entitled to 14 days notice of the call, and joint holders of a share are jointly and severally liable to pay the call[1]. Where a call has been made but not yet paid, it may be revoked in whole or in part, and payment of a call may be revoked in whole or in part. A person on whom a call is made remains liable for the call even if he subsequently transfers his shares.

1 Table A, reg 14.

5.76 A number of problems may be seen to arise from the wording of this regulation. First, it is not clear whether the directors can be selective in making calls. Presumably, if shares have been issued partly paid at different times there need be no objection to making calls on some and not others. What of the position where shares have been issued partly paid at the same time, but to different persons. Can the directors then make calls on some of the allottees and not on others? On the face of it, the answer must be that they can do this, but this opens an obvious possibility for abuse, since the directors could choose to make calls on shareholders whom they knew to be unable to afford to pay, in order to put themselves in a position to forfeit those shares. This could in turn affect the balance of power within the company to the advantage of the directors. It is in effect a way of circumventing the rules on pre-emption rights, although it may be observed that it is to that extent merely a variant of the well-known device of offering shares to the shareholders pro rata to their existing holdings at a time when the directors know that not all will be able to take up the offer. It is therefore suggested that the proper answer to this is the same as that applicable to initial allotments in the same circumstances, namely that the power to allot shares is a fiduciary power of the directors and must be exercised bona fide and in the best interests of the company.

5.77 The second question concerns the position of the allottee who transfers after the call is made. It is clear that if the transferee pays the call, the transferor's liability ceases. In addition, if the transferee pays the call in order to avoid forfeiture, it is to be presumed that the transferee is then able to recover the amount of the call from the transferor. Finally, the transferor and transferee could agree as between themselves that the liability to pay the call falls on the transferee (this presumably being reflected in the price) but such an agreement cannot affect the company's right to proceed against the transferor. To hold otherwise would be to allow the transferor to assign the burden of the contract without the consent of the obligee, and it is well settled that English law does not permit this.

5.78 Regulation 13 of Table A provides that calls are deemed to have been made at the time when the resolution of the directors authorising the call is passed. Thus, the 14 days for the payment of the call run from that time.

5.79 Table A, regulation 15 deals with the consequences of failure to pay a call within the 14 days allowed by regulation 12. The outstanding sum carries interest from the expiry of the 14 days until the date of payment. The rate may be fixed by the terms of allotment, or by the notice of call (though the terms of allotment would presumably prevail in the event of any conflict). If neither of these specifies a rate of interest, then the applicable rate is that laid down by the Act. Regulation 15 authorises the directors to waive the interest in whole or in part.

5.80 The provisions relating to calls apply equally to an amount payable in respect of a share on allotment or a date fixed at the date of allotment. A case on the giving of notice in relation to proposed forfeitures is *Parkstone Ltd v Gulf Guarantee Bank plc*[1]. The company sent a letter to the holder of partly-paid shares giving notice that unless the shareholder paid the calls due on the shares it would forfeit them. The notice was sent to the shareholder's registered address in Gibraltar notwithstanding that the shareholder had informed the company of an address in London for the service of notices. The company's articles of association included reg 131 of Table A in Sch 1 to the Companies Act 1948. It was held that under regulation 131 of Table A in Sch 1 to the 1948 Act a company could choose whether to give notice to a member 'personally', 'by sending it by post to him', 'by sending it by post . . . to his registered address' or, in the case of a member who had no registered address within the United Kingdom but who had supplied to the company an address within the United Kingdom for the giving of notice, by sending it by post to that address. Accordingly, the company's notice had been effectively served on the shareholder.

1 [1990] BCLC 850, [1990] BCC 534, ChD.

Chapter 6

Conclusions: the regulation of share capital

6.1 The rules dealt with in this book are without doubt detailed and complex. They have been formed over a period of more than a century, and it is probably fair to say that they have never been subjected to any systematic review. This is therefore an opportune point at which to examine the rules as a regulatory structure. In doing this it is pertinent to ask three questions:

- does the system appear to have a rational set of objectives?
- does it pursue those objectives in a logical and internally consistent way?
- is the system free of unnecessary complexity and bureaucracy?

DOES THE SYSTEM APPEAR TO HAVE A RATIONAL SET OF OBJECTIVES?

6.2 It is worth observing at this point that it is far from easy to discern any clear set of objectives behind the various rules dealing with share capital. In a fashion typical of the development of English law they have grown up in a piecemeal fashion, often in response to particular perceived problems. Any attempt to list the objectives of the rules is unlikely to be anything more than an *ex post facto* rationalisation of a structure which is in fact incoherent.

6.3 The basic principle of capital maintenance, from which all the rules in this area may be regarded as being derived, may be regarded as still retaining some validity in the sense that now, as 140 years ago, it is legitimate to suggest that creditors want some degree of assurance of the financial solidity of the company with which they deal. On the other hand the deficiencies of this basic theory have already been alluded to. First, there is no assurance that a private company will have more than the most nominal limited capital. Second, it is unrealistic to imagine that anyone really enquires as to the authorised or issued capital of a company before dealing with it. Third, even where the issued capital is quite large, it is in practice often tied up in illiquid assets, so that it does not in any real sense offer a fund against which the creditor can claim.

6.4 Historically, it may be said that the idea of minimum capital was part of the price paid for limited liability, but this trade-off must appear largely obsolete in an environment where limited liability has come to be seen as a right rather than a privilege. Moreover, it is fairly obvious that the present rules allow for significant derogations from the capital maintenance principle, not least in relation to financial assistance for the purchase of shares and share buy-back.

6.5 In view of the above it is perhaps time to say that the objectives of the rules on share capital should be recast. Arguably, such a recasting would be no more than a belated recognition of the premises underlying the rules which now exist. It is suggested that these objectives might be presented as being something along the following lines, to contribute to the holding of an appropriate balance among the various interest groups within the company; in particular:

1. *To protect existing shareholders from the forced depletion of their interest in the company, either by the dilution of that interest or by its devaluation.* This is an objective which clearly is recognised by the existing rules requiring directors to be authorised before issuing share capital, and by those rules which provide for pre-emption rights for existing shareholders on the issuing of new capital. It is a curious thing that these rules date only from 1980 and were introduced only in response to an EU Directive, but they do now form part of English law. Apart from these statutory rules, English law had of course developed more general notions of the protection of shareholders, both by cases such as Hogg v Cramphorn[1] and by more general notions of oppressive conduct of the majority.

2. *To protect the company as an entity from being looted by unscrupulous shareholders or promoters.* The importance of this objective cannot seriously be disputed. However, rules on share capital can play only a relatively small part in achieving it. Certainly the history of company law has many examples of unscrupulous directors who paid the company's capital in the form of dividends in order to keep their shareholders happy[2], and the rules against the distribution of dividends other than out of distributable profits make such behaviour more difficult at the present day. At the same time there are many ways in which dishonest directors and controllers can take money out of a company without infringing the rules on protection of share capital.

3. *To protect creditors from the unjustified diminution of the value of the company's assets against which they would be able to enforce their claims (though without accepting a formal equivalence between issued share capital and asset values).* Clearly creditors do have a legitimate interest in the continuing financial viability of the company, though it is equally clear that English law generally does not recognise them as having a legally protected interest in corporate management and governance, so long as the company is able to pay its debts as they fall due. This is another area where the major forms of protective legislation do not directly relate to the maintenance of share capital. Directors are exposed to potential civil and criminal liability for negligently[3] or fraudulently[4] failing to manage the company in a proper way, and may also become liable to disqualification[5] if the company

subsequently fails. Although the depletion of the company's capital is something which could properly be taken into account in any of these proceedings, it is neither a necessary nor a sufficient condition for the imposition of liability.

It hardly needs to be added that this formulation leaves many vital questions unanswered. The issue of where the appropriate balance between the different interests is to be found is of course the fundamental ongoing controversy of company law, and the formulation given here cannot by itself resolve that problem. In addition, the three more particular objectives identified above may to some extent be mutually conflicting, as well as being in themselves somewhat imprecise.

1 [1967] Ch 254, [1966] 3 All ER 420.

2 Some of the best-known offenders were the great railway barons of the nineteenth century such as George Hudson. See for example Kostal RW, *Law and English Railway Capitalism 1825-75* (1997).

3 IA 1986, s 214.

4 IA 1986, s 213 (civil liability); CA 1985, s 458 (criminal liability).

5 Company Directors Disqualification Act 1986.

DOES THE SYSTEM PURSUE THOSE OBJECTIVES IN A LOGICAL AND INTERNALLY CONSISTENT WAY?

6.6 It is of course unfair to judge the present system against the objectives outlined above, since it is clearly not at present pursuing those objectives. A major criticism of the present system is that it no longer appears to have any clarity about which objectives it is in fact pursuing. The nineteenth century capital maintenance doctrine has been significantly watered down in a number of respects, but the law has not been prepared formally to abandon it, far less to look for anything coherent to put in its place. The lack of coherence is of course aggravated by the fact that some of the present rules were enacted in response to EU Directives. This has at least two problematic effects. First, the substance of some of the rules does not necessarily sit easily with the conceptual underpinnings of English law. Second, in some cases the legislator has simply copied the wording of the English version of the Directives, apparently without adequate consideration of their meaning or of how they fit with the rest of the legislation. A non-specialist lawyer attempting to make sense of the resulting statutory sections may experience considerable difficulty.

IS THE SYSTEM FREE OF UNNECESSARY COMPLEXITY AND BUREAUCRACY?

6.7 It is inevitable that under this heading the present system will score very badly. The complexities of a number of areas of the existing rules has already been mentioned.

6.8 The history of the rules on financial assistance for the purchase of a company's own shares is not a happy one. Before 1981 such assistance was more or less absolutely prohibited. Since then the rules have been relaxed somewhat, though only subject to the need to comply with procedural safeguards of a very technical character. Such limited case law as there is in this area since 1981 suggests that the rules continue to constitute a trap for the unwary, capable of defeating perfectly reasonable and sensible transactions without necessarily catching those transactions which are in reality likely to have harmful effects.

6.9 Similar points may perhaps be made about the rules on buy-back of shares, though these at least do not appear to place insuperable obstacles in the way of a company wishing to carry out such transactions.

6.10 The rules on issue of new shares may probably be considered unreasonably technical in many places. The discussion earlier in this work of the procedures relating to non-cash consideration for the issue of shares has highlighted the extent to which the rules pose technical obstacles which are at best disproportionate to the objectives being pursued and at worst irrelevant to those objectives.

6.11 Although there are significant differences between the rules for private companies and the rules for public companies, it may be suggested that the share capital rules for private companies are probably still too restrictive.

6.12 Part of the problem may be said to be that shares in companies perform a number of overlapping but not identical functions. They represent the capital contributions made by members. They determine the division of ownership within the company (in practice this means that they determine rights to dividends and to participate in surplus capital on a winding up). They determine the voting rights of the members in those cases where effective decision-making power remains vested in the members in General Meeting. The obvious difficulty is that there are many cases where it would be desirable to have these three aspects of the company divided in different ways. There is of course no great logical difficulty in achieving such a split – the idea of class rights exists in part to solve exactly such cases. The problem with this approach is twofold. First, it takes a positive effort to create class rights, the presumption being that all three aspects are sliced in exactly the same way. Second, the introduction of class rights then produces such complexity and difficulty that many practitioners are put off the very idea.

6.13 In truth, at least part of this complexity is unavoidable – if there are to be class rights, then those rights have to be protected in some way, since the class rights were created for a purpose, and the law should not readily allow that purpose to be evaded. On the other hand, the enormous added burden of working out the relationship between where the rights are granted and where the amendment provisions are to be found adds a wholly unnecessary layer of complexity.

6.14 There would seem to be merit in the production of some standard forms for share classes, which might conveniently be adopted by most companies wanting to have class rights. The existence of these forms would not of course preclude the development of more elaborate forms in those cases where they were commercially necessary. Of possibly greater importance is the simplification of the procedures for altering class rights. Again it would seem desirable to offer companies a limited range of alteration procedures. These would probably not differ greatly from those currently in use. The refinements would be that the procedures would be more clearly spelt out and that it would become more difficult to challenge changes made in accordance with those procedures.

SUGGESTIONS FOR REFORM

6.15 This is the most difficult part of this chapter to write. It is easy enough to bemoan the very obvious shortcomings of the present rules, but much less easy to come to any view as to what should be done about them. The following suggestions are intended to point the way to a system more suited to the 21st century.

6.16 First, it must be accepted that there is a major difference in this area between private companies and public companies, especially listed companies. In private companies the problem of share capital should be seen as essentially a private matter between the shareholders. The lack of any minimum capital requirement makes it unrealistic and unreasonable to suggest that creditors have any legitimate interest in the question (this is not to impugn those rules which require directors to manage the company properly – it merely makes the point that these rules have really nothing to do with the topic of share capital). On the other hand, share capital questions do have a good deal to do with control within private companies.

6.17 Of the possible objectives identified above for the rules on share capital, only the first can really be considered relevant in private companies. For reasons already given, those rules would benefit from some further revision. The major provisions of ss 80 and 89 of the CA 1985 cannot of course be substantially altered because they are derived from the Second Company Law Directive. In any event the substance of these rules is unobjectionable, though some clarification of the circumstances in which the pre-emption rights can be excluded would be welcome.

6.18 Although the use of class rights within companies is not as common as it was, the analysis above of the differing uses to which share capital can be put suggests that it would be beneficial if class rights could be used more frequently in order to distinguish these uses. That in turn points to the need for reform and clarification of the rules for creating and amending class rights. The present rules are unnecessarily complex in procedural terms, whilst at the same time undesirably vague from the point of view of identifying exactly what rights are protected and in what circumstances these rights can be altered. These rules pre-date the current version of the general minority protection rules in s 459 of the CA 1985, and it may be suggested that any amendment should take account of this by applying expressly the s 459 tests to any objection to alteration of class rights[1]. Indeed, the extensive development of the power of the court to protect minorities has now gone so far that it is questionable whether any other specific provision is needed in narrower areas of company law. Although the subsuming of objections to changes of class rights within the CA 1985, s 459 jurisdiction might be though to promote uncertainty, there is no reason why this should be so. The existing power of the court is discretionary, and the existing case law on CA 1985, s 127 could continue to be used as a guide to the approach to be taken in such cases.

1 CA 1985, s 126 expressly declares that the procedure for objecting to changes of class rights has no effect on the possibility of a s 459 application.

6.19 In relation to public companies the arguments are of course somewhat different. This is partly because of the larger economic scale on which these companies generally operate and partly, in the case of listed companies, because of the need to preserve and enhance public confidence in the market. These are essentially the arguments which justify the use of minimum capital requirements and controls on non-cash consideration for the issue of shares, two sets of rules which apply only to public companies. Beyond these areas the Companies Acts do little to impose extra rules on the share capital of public companies, though attention is drawn in CA 1985, ss 454–457 on the possibility of disenfranchising shares where the beneficial ownership of these shares is not disclosed. The other major question arising in relation to the shares of such companies concerns the arrangements for transferring ownership. So far as the law is concerned there is no difference between private and public companies in this regard. The practical differences are derived entirely from the existence and practices of the Stock Market itself. These rules have of course developed substantially in recent years, but the changes have come about as a result of the need to take account of technological developments (notably the electronic recording of share ownership) rather than because of fundamental problems of investor protection.

THE FUTURE

6.20 It can hardly be said that the subject of share capital is one where there is at present significant pressure for reform. The earlier chapters of this book have highlighted a number of areas where the law is either unclear or somewhat problematic, yet for the most part practitioners appear to find ways of circumventing such problems as exist. Some modest improvements could usefully be effected, but it is fairly clear that major reforms are not possible without undermining much of the conceptual structure upon which company law is based. Nor is it clear that major reforms are necessary or even desirable.

Index